W9-CDB-898

The
Pursuit of
American Character

The
Pursuit of
American Character

RUPERT WILKINSON

EMERSON COLLEGE LIBRARY

1817

HARPER & ROW, PUBLISHERS, NEW YORK

CAMBRIDGE, PHILADELPHIA, SAN FRANCISCO, WASHINGTON
LONDON, MEXICO CITY, SÃO PAULO, SINGAPORE, SYDNEY

E
169.1
.W489
1988

For Mary

THE PURSUIT OF AMERICAN CHARACTER. Copyright © 1988 by Rupert Wilkinson. All rights reserved. Printed in the United States of America. No part of this book may be used or reproduced in any manner whatsoever without written permission except in the case of brief quotations embodied in critical articles and reviews. For information address Harper & Row, Publishers, Inc., 10 E. 53rd Street, New York, N.Y. 10022. Published simultaneously in Canada by Fitzhenry & Whiteside Ltd., Toronto.

FIRST EDITION

Designed by Erich Hobbing

Library of Congress Cataloging-in-Publication Data
Wilkinson, Rupert.
  The pursuit of American character.

  (Icon editions)
  Bibliography: p.
  Includes index.
  1. National characteristics, American. 2. United States—Civilization. I. Title.
E169.1.W489 1988   973   87-46182
ISBN 0-06-438876-X
ISBN 0-06-430180-X (pbk.)

---

88 89 90 91 92 AC/HC 10 9 8 7 6 5 4 3 2 1

Contents

Preface

At the core of this book's material is a literature, a stream of books and essays on American social character, written mainly by historians and social scientists who have put aside the specialized monograph and have generalized about the attitudes and values of a modern people. Imaginative and aware as these writers were, I believe they said more than they realized. Inevitably their judgment was affected by the particular times in which they wrote; but their work also has a timelessness, expressing concerns and anxieties old in American culture.

This book therefore has a double focus. I am interested in the *pursuit* of American character—the effort to identify and pin it down—as a way of understanding American character itself.

I must add a special word about Chapter 2. It reviews the above literature between the early 1940s and mid-1980s. All the modern classics on American character are there, from Margaret Mead, *And Keep Your Powder Dry* (1942), through David Riesman et al., *The Lonely Crowd* (1950), and Christopher Lasch, *The Culture of Narcissism* (1979). I have tried here to write a guide that will be of value in its own right; to summarize as sensitively as I can a changing commentary on American character against a changing historical background. I do not encompass all that the writers say, or fully convey how they say it. But I do want to avoid the usual approach of intellectual historians who cite selectively from their 'principals' without laying out their arguments end to end.

I can deviate from this norm because the literature is manageable: about thirty statements (most of them by well-known authors) say all there is to say. I have omitted from these a few studies whose conclusions largely overlap the ones discussed; I also omit studies that simply list 'American' traits without much explanation or connection, or (more usefully) concentrate on just one tendency. All these will be mentioned in a sequel to this book, an anthology of modern writing on American social character. The anthology will include a critical assessment of these studies and a detailed bibliographical essay tracing the passage of various ideas.

Parts of the first two chapters of this book first appeared in the *Journal of American Studies* (vol. 17, August 1983), published by Cambridge University Press. The general idea of a new, short book on American character originated with Cass Canfield, Jr., at Harper & Row. I much appreciate his encouragement at every stage and his constructive comments on the text. I am also grateful to Marjorie Horvitz at Harper's for her sensitive, all-seeing copy-editing; and to Craig Comstock, agent, adviser, and generous friend. A number of colleagues and students at Sussex University and Smith College helped me develop and refine my ideas—I acknowledge them more specifically in the notes.

In the middle of writing this book I switched from using an Imperial portable typewriter (aptly trade-named "The Good Companion," for it had served me from the 1950s) to an Atari word-processor. To call this event a technological trauma may strike younger readers as precious and pathetic; but that is what it was. I thank Leila Burrell-Davis, Liz Hinton, Mayer Wantman, and Matthew Fender for guiding me with patience and clarity to the magic slopes of Silicon Valley. I appreciate, too, the cheerful aid given me by Marion Cox in turning the old typescript into printout and checking the last few details.

The dedication of this book to my wife, Mary, can only begin to express my debt to her. Despite a stressful and demanding job, and more than her due share of physical pain and domestic worries, she spent many hours on the first draft. With the astringency of the good journalist and editor she is, she challenged me to tell my complex tale as simply and directly as I could. Her support was critical in both senses.

February 1988

∗   ∗   ∗

Note on quotation marks: Double quotes are used throughout the text for quotations from specific writers or speakers. Single quotes denote colloquialisms or revealing clichés.

1

An Industry

From the Revolution to the present, Americans have displayed an enormous interest in assessing their social character. Today that interest is a national tradition, supporting an august industry of books and articles on what it means to be an American. When the historian Christopher Lasch published *The Minimal Self* in 1984, it was his *second* book on psychological dimensions of individualism in America, and part of a continuing debate. In no other country can one imagine a leading social historian devoting so much of his work to the collective psyche of his contemporaries.[1]

A lot of Lasch's writing does not make it clear if he is decrying specifically American trends or a more general condition of 'modern man.' This ambiguity is not his alone. Many Americans believe that, on a personal plane at least, they are particularly classless, democratic, and individualist; yet some of them also believe that American-style democracy and individualism can grow almost anywhere and can be demanded of regimes they don't like (especially communist ones). Even educated Americans often do not know what is distinctive about their culture and what is basically shared with others.

Ironically, the spate of books and articles in the late 1970s and early '80s depicting a new American egoism obscured the question of what was American about it. By declaring a sea change in values and behavior, they usually compared American character with that character in the past rather than the character of other peoples. Yet these studies were still part of the tradition, the historic search for a national psychological identity. Why Americans, far more than others, have attracted such study is a question that scholars have seldom addressed and have inadequately answered.

From these thoughts came the three purposes of this essay. The first purpose is to look at the whole nature of the search for American character; to ask what has propelled that search; and to suggest that although the enterprise has recruited foreign writers, it is itself a significant aspect of American culture and character. Second, I wish to take stock of the studies of American character that have poured out between the 1940s and the 1980s—to see what has changed and what has not in the writers' concerns.

My third aim is to try to give a fresh perspective on individualism, community, and conformity, subjects that have beset these writers. I want to show that the dual attraction of Americans to individualism and to 'getting together' has always been exceedingly complex. There are different kinds of American individualism; there are different kinds of 'getting together'; and the two are not always polar opposites. Above all, I wish to discuss four historic American fears that have surrounded this dual attraction: the fear of *being owned* (including fears of dependence and of being controlled and shaped by others); the fear of *falling apart* (a fear of anarchy and isolation); the fear of *winding down* (losing energy, dynamism, forward motion); and the fear of *falling away* from a past virtue and promise.

The four fears include worries about oneself as well as society, and about the state of community as well as the state of individualism. Sometimes they reinforce each other and sometimes they conflict, but in one form or another I believe they account for much of the appeal of the voluminous writing about American character—again, the search for an American character is part of that character.

This is not to suggest that Americans spend their lives in trembling misery. A little fear is necessary to survival and a spice to more positive emotions. I do not claim that Americans are more or less fearful than others; it is the shape and direction of their fears that is the issue.

In examining historically rooted attitudes, I deliberately focus on what is traditional in American culture. Of course, America has undergone an enormous amount of change during its history. Social commentators and historians, however, often seek attention by discovering and exaggerating a 'revolution' in this or that aspect of society. Culture, in any event, is not all of a piece: some elements change more than others. Although the four fears have appeared in different forms and intensities at different times, and although they are shaped by changing economic and social circumstances, much of their force derives from traditional ideas and values that have a life of their own, that are not simply determined by economic structures.

Let us start with definitions. By 'social character,' or 'American social character,' I mean those traits of individual personality and attitude that the population shows more frequently or in different ways than other, compared populations do. It is therefore a highly relative concept. Any population's social character must always depend partly on what other populations it is being compared with, explicitly or implicitly. My own standard of comparison for American character is with people in other modern industrial countries.

The concept of social character overlaps that of 'culture.' By 'culture' I simply mean here a shared way of life: those attitudes and procedures that members of a population share and transmit to each other. Social character operates at culture's most personal pole, though some theories of social character are more deeply psychological than others. Essentially they divide between conceptions of a core personality structure, embedded in the unconscious and largely established in childhood; and theories that confine themselves to a more conscious set of attitudes and values. In neither case, however, does social character embrace all of a person's traits; some will be his or hers alone.

Using the notion of social character requires a certain common sense. Suppose a population contains a section of people—large compared to its equivalents elsewhere but still thin on the ground—who commit murder and other acts of violence. It does not follow that the whole population has a violent social character. It only makes sense to say this if the violence of the minority finds some resonance and support in the culture and underlying attitudes of numerous people in the whole population. A common misuse of the concept is to attribute a set of social-character tendencies to a larger population than is justified—to declare as 'American' what in fact are the traits only of middle-class Americans, say, or American males, or big-city easterners.

On the other hand, the fact that a social-character tendency is bound to differ in form and intensity according to class, sex, region, etc., does not automatically preclude it from characterizing to some extent a complex national population. In the 1950s, James Baldwin described his "astonishment" at discovering, as a black writer in Paris, how *American* he felt, for all his feelings of isolation from his countrymen, black as well as white. His discovery was a powerful recognition of the force of national character.[2]

My own thinking about four historic fears in American social character deliberately stresses middle- and upper-class attitudes. Two of the four fears are apt to thrive where people have education and means for the 'higher' worries. Nothing so encourages a fear of falling away as the rather abstract concept of a mission laid upon Americans by their past; and the fear of winding down is often sharpest where people have *careers,* that is, occupations built on the expectation of moving up ('professional development,' as the euphemism has it). Manual and service workers seldom have careers in this sense (few will make supervisor). The annual pay raise, admittedly, may involve workers in a sense of failure and winding down if it does not materialize or does not outstrip inflation; but in these groups job security is likely to be more important than 'moving ahead.'

The passion for *corporate growth* too—the notion that a company falls back if it stands still—impinges more directly on the lives and attitudes of executives and professionals and their families than further down the class scale. By contrast, the fear and dislike of being owned, of being controlled and pushed around by bosses and systems, is strong among manual workers; and run-down neighborhoods, ethnic conflicts, and other social strains make many lower-class people no strangers to the fear of falling apart.

The four fears are not, however, just the product of class experience. They express basic human anxieties about corruption, impotence, and chaos; at the same time, the distinctive nature of American history has enabled the four fears to resonate through the nation's culture and to color populist as well as 'establishment' political language.

Between the early 1940s and the mid-1980s, at least twenty books were published on American social character. This is an average of almost one book every two years (in fact there was a lull in publishing on American character in the late sixties and much of the seventies), and my count excludes articles and parts of other books on the same subject, as well as more general works on American social trends. Many, perhaps most, middle-class Americans know none of these studies, but several have been big sellers—especially David Riesman's *The Lonely Crowd* (1950), William Whyte's *The Organization Man* (1956), Charles Reich's *The Greening of America* (1970), and Christopher Lasch's *The Culture of Narcissism* (1979)—though Riesman's and Lasch's books were not particularly easy to read.

Only the pace of this output is new. The all-time most-cited thesis by an American historian—Frederick Jackson Turner's paper of 1893 on "The Significance of the Frontier in American History"—is partly a statement about American social character.[3] The all-time most-cited work on America by a foreigner—Alexis de Tocqueville's *Democracy in America* (1835)—is even more a statement about American social character. It is still virtually de rigueur to cite Tocqueville at some point during a college course on the American nineteenth century and in the many courses that deal with notions of American individualism.

And yet we have a paradox. Despite the development of attitude surveys and interview techniques, social scientists and historians have often regarded theories of social character, especially national character, as 'soft' generalizations. They run against scholarly, and American, standards of tangible, 'show me' evidence. As a result, work on American social character has tended to be the capstone of a sociologist's or historian's career made in a different field. This is less true of the psychoanalytic anthropologists led in the 1940s by Margaret Mead and Geoffrey Gorer; and it is not at all true of David Riesman, who has made the study of American character into a gigantic career project, along with his work on the history and sociology of higher education. Generally speaking, though, the study of American social character is not an established career specialty for either historians or social scientists.

Not that this matters in the popular and 'middle-brow' media. Taking the national pulse is a recurring pastime for newspapers and magazines. What is 'the nation's mood'? What changes are under way in Americans' attitudes to themselves, their work, other people, the future? 'New findings show that seven out of ten Americans . . .'

All this is made more respectable by articles and books on the attitudes and styles of particular groups—football players, managers, southern women. Gender issues, too, have promoted commentary on group attitudes and feelings, not just in books but in magazines ranging from *Psychology Today* to *U.S. News & World Report*.[4]

The American fascination with social character showed up in the laments of the late 1970s and early '80s about the country's 'economic decline,' the discovery by many commentators that the nation's 'edge' over other economies was narrowing and that U.S. productivity was growing more and more slowly (a trend sometimes confused with absolute decline). Some of these writers saw the problem almost immediately as a 'failure of nerve,' the loss of will to win. They jumped with ease from identifying a new pessimism about the *nation's* future to implying that Americans were losing confidence in themselves *personally*. Opinion surveys that challenged or qualified these conclusions still dealt in the same social-psychological coin.[5]

The British, too, have blamed their failures on cultural attitudes, but they have produced less discussion in this vein, and it has taken them a much longer period of economic decline to do so. What criticism there has been of social attitudes has often concentrated on particular classes and joined with a critique of institutions such as Britain's elite 'public schools.' The public schools have been attacked on two fronts: on the left, for dividing the country and so impeding cooperation; on the right, for perpetuating a gentlemanly disdain of heavy industry and commercial enterprise.

Strangely enough, in a country that tends to shun psychological explanations of itself, no one relies on them more than that economic materialist Margaret Thatcher, who projects no vision of community. She believes instead in a basically individualist human nature, which responds to simple rewards and punishments but can also acquire, through bad habits and false indoctrination, a weak and dependent social character. Convinced that basic attitudes must be reversed, Thatcher has required little evidence to maintain her faith that tax-cut "incentives" propel producers into hard work and enterprise, for her faith is founded on a simple view of human nature.

Thatcher's accompanying belief that government programs and state welfare create habits of dependency is part of a conservative tradition that has flourished since the nineteenth century on both sides of the Atlantic. Quite recently, too, discussions of the 'British Disease'—linking it to social attitudes that allegedly discourage hard work, business dynamism, and the use of technology—have come from American as well as British writers and have made comparisons with American character. In other words, resorting to social character to explain the British predicament is a partly American enterprise.[6]

Another Anglo-American comparison lies in the parallel between post–Boer War Britain and post–Vietnam War America, between British doubts about the validity of the Empire and the future of the imperial spirit and American anxieties about the nation's 'will' and world position. In the early 1900s, Germany's competitive economic power—like Japan for America today—inflamed British concerns about a *fin-de-siècle* decline and the state of national morale.

Yet then, as later, vivid class differences inhibited the effort to generalize about a British national character. (So perhaps did the value placed on psychological privacy by this densely packed people.) From Charles Masterman's *The Condition of England* in 1909 to George Orwell's "England Your England" in 1942 to Geoffrey Gorer's work in the 1950s, writers on Britain have shown in different ways how hard it is for a conception of social character to cross class lines.[7]

All nations, of course, have class differences, but in Britain they are particularly visible—and audible. This may explain why interpreters of Australian society, where class seems less important, can generalize nationally about 'mateship' and the effect of outback myths (while in fact focusing largely on males). So it is with America. The assumption that the society lacks strong class barriers and is largely 'middle class' has encouraged both natives and foreigners to generalize about American character. This, however, only helps explain why they feel *able* to do so. We must now ask what has *impelled* them to do so and for so long, in the face of formidable geographic and ethnic differences.

To understand the American character industry we must start with early visitors and immigrants. What made them generalize about Americans?

To begin with, America was the most dramatic child of their ancestors' imaginings—wayward or promising, like but unlike. Set in a romantic landscape, it was an experiment in new social relationships, a test of what would happen when an old mold was broken and remade, mostly with familiar materials. Above all, it was a test of democracy. At times European onlookers showed a strong wish to 'pathologize' Americans. In 1814, an article in London's *Quarterly Review* targeted on the United States the writer's fear of radical "jacobinism." By declaring that Americans had come under "Gallic" cultural influence (not just French political influence), he could assert that America was fundamentally diseased and noxious, however benign its policies might seem.[8]

So the sense that America was special and (for better or worse) exemplary was not just a product of native cultural nationalism; it was also a direct projection by foreigners upon the New World. Americans, in return, developed favorable self-portraits in defense against the more unflattering of the foreigners' reports. Untidily, however, the foreign and the native blurred together, as foreign-born commentators became American residents, from Crèvecoeur in the late eighteenth century to Hugo Münsterberg in the late nineteenth.

A similar interaction has occurred in our own time. The range of modern U.S. power in the world—cultural as well as economic and political—has made American attitudes and behavior a topic of international interest, while Americans often want to know—as they always have—what foreigners think of them. When the Italian writer Luigi Barzini published an essay on "The American" in *Harper's Magazine* (December 1981), his American editors attached the subhead "Why We Baffle the Europeans," though the piece was not mainly on that theme.*

Early American society developed its concern with social character in three stages. First, in colonial New England, the *Puritan task,* the idea of a "special commission" from God to build a Christian commonwealth, required a people to reassess constantly their spiritual

---

*In hiring outside advice to get the 'big picture,' American corporations too can look abroad. In the early 1980s, American Express and other firms paid $20,000 each for a study of U.S. socio-economic trends and changing attitudes by a consortium of British social scientists. Advertised to other corporations and individuals in 1985 as a limited-supply "confidential document" at $285, it subsequently became a trade book (1987 price, $19.95). Oxford Analytica, *America in Perspective: Major Trends in the United States through the 1980s* (Boston, 1986).

and social progress, or lack of it. Second, the assertion of *republican-ism* contained the belief that democracy depended on the virtue of the people and their resistance to foreign corruptions—all the more as their nation was explicitly founded on a set of moral and political principles. Third, the anxieties of *cultural nationalism* before the Civil War impelled Americans to find qualities in themselves that bound them together while distinguishing them from their parent civilizations.[9]

Two modern factors, really bundles of factors, have extended Americans' interest in their character. The first I will call *psychology writ large;* the second, *intellectual Americanism.*

Psychology writ large involves two arguments. The first is that Americans, because of their population size, GNP, and economic development, tend to produce more of everything—including more scholarship, more social science, and, within that, more study of social character. The second argument asserts that the first is true but insufficient. Americans have been specially drawn to many branches of psychology (including psychoanalysis) as well as sociology; and the study of social character provides bridges between psychology, sociology, and, indeed, history.

It is significant that psychoanalysis, the most inward branch of psychology, has flourished in America as nowhere else. In its American forms, however, it has also looked outward. From Harry Stack Sullivan to Erik Erikson, some of the country's most famous psychologists have combined psychoanalytic insights with attention to social relations. But why have Americans been so attracted to psychological thinking and language? The language, of course, does not always go with much thinking; but many reasons come to mind, and all of them predate the 1970s "Me Decade," in which Americans supposedly became more interested in their own psyches.

- *Burdens of individualism.* When a culture demands that each person feel happy as well as successful, people are attracted to self-engineering, taking oneself in hand, to ward off anxiety and failure.[10]
- *The Puritan legacy.* Even though it was diluted and secularized, Puritanism left a tradition of introspection, self-improvement, and collective as well as personal self-criticism.

• *Intellectual democracy* (or the 'intellectualization of the mundane'). From their first settlements, Americans tended to erode gentlemanly distinctions between academic and applied ideas. Today, in the great universe of U.S. higher education, virtually no subject is deemed unworthy of a degree, somewhere. In self-help and 'how-to' books, no aspect of personal and everyday life is considered beneath (or above) popular analysis. Anyone can learn auto mechanics; anyone can be his own psychologist.

• *Friction and movement.* A kaleidoscopic society with many people leaving home and moving about puts a premium on learning how to relate to others and relearning one's own identity. Psychology offers guidance and reassurance when one's 'folks' are far away.

• *Motivating the employee.* In large organizations, where people seldom see the end result of their work, 'motivation' becomes a problem, and industrial and personnel psychologists find a market.

• *Reaching the customer/voter.* In commercial marketing and electoral politics alike, campaign managers have to study attitudes and emotions. By the 1920s, the use of social psychology in mass advertising was common, but survey techniques have greatly developed since then. In two prescient novels, *The Ninth Wave* (1956) and *The 480* (1964), Eugene Burdick described the sophisticated targeting of voters in key social-psychological constituencies— categories defined by attitudes as well as sociological traits. Much of this has come about, in marketing as well as politics.

What unites this list? Historically, it represents a meeting point of Puritan, democratic, and capitalist traditions, plus problems of mass organization and the affluence and time to get worried about the self. Psychologically, it combines a wish to develop and express the self with the drive to be effective in the outside world; it contains likewise the pursuit of individual distinctiveness and a compensating search for community. These themes are old in American consciousness. The emphases change, but the fascination with 'self and society,' with the tensions and nourishments between the two, is an enduring part of the culture, and a powerful element in the fascination with national character.

The second modern force behind the American social-character industry is *intellectual Americanism*: the wish to identify and make much of American ways. This motive helps explain the whole tendency of Americans to produce general interpretations of their culture and society, whether or not they are focused on social character. Intellectual Americanism connects most obviously with studies that stress the uniqueness of the American experience. It also, however, fuels those theories that attribute a changing American character to socioeconomic trends in the modern world at large, for these theories, too, give America a special place, as the advance guard of wider trends.

What drives intellectual Americanism? The historian David Potter suggested that Americans went in search of their national character because of their immigrant backgrounds; they felt themselves to be a society of newcomers, unbonded by a common ethnic heritage.[11] Yet other nations of immigrants have not made such a fuss about their character. It is more likely that America's unique *mixture* of centrifugal traits—no other country is *at once* so ethnically and geographically varied, so physically big, so subject to urban and technical change—has impelled Americans to ask: 'Who are we?' 'What holds us together?' 'What are we becoming?' And if the signs are bad, if the social-character prophets declare that Americans are becoming "organization men" or self-isolated consumers or aggressive narcissists, then at least one can be what David Riesman called the "inside dopester": can believe one has the key to the behavior of others and feel superior.[12]

So even when the findings are unfavorable to American character (as is often the case), they provide reassurance amid change, and all the more so when society and the world seem ungovernable; if events cannot be controlled politically, they can still be managed cognitively. Some studies of American character reassure by stressing continuity; they identify traditional values and attitudes that allegedly have survived socioeconomic change. Other studies classify change in American character itself, and so provide a road map through a bewildering succession of styles and attitudes.

Just as psychology writ large reflects a dual concern with individualism and affiliation, so intellectual Americanism expresses the four fears that weave through this concern. The search for a shared American character answers a fear of falling apart; it also speaks to fears of falling away, of winding down, and, in subtle ways, of being owned. A lot of writing on the national character since World War II has suggested that Americans have lost historic qualities, including industriousness, authenticity, and spiritual independence.

Admittedly even the works that stress change in American character do not agree on what has been lost, or gained; nor do they uncritically glorify the past or totally despair of the future. I cannot claim, anyway, that all four fears have driven every writer on American character. I do claim that the fears, and the hopes that form their positive counterpart, are part of the culture.[13]

2

A Literature

Between the 1940s and the 1980s, writing on American character made a U-turn. It moved from stressing the effects of social pressure and conformity to worries about an unstable, isolating egoism. The shift, however, was not simple. Among all the writers there were continuities as well as differences.

The best-known of the 1940s vintage are Margaret Mead's *And Keep Your Powder Dry: An Anthropologist Looks at America* (1942) and Geoffrey Gorer's *The American People* (1948). They survive best today because they were fresh then—the bold if crude efforts of anthropologists to stress the effects of child-rearing practices while locating them in long-lasting historical and social conditions.

Margaret Mead's book was a direct product of World War II, written with speed and verve in the summer following Pearl Harbor. Mead was one of a bevy of anthropologists recruited by the U.S. government to study aspects of wartime living, propaganda, and morale (enemy as well as Allied). An ardent internationalist, she wrote the book to enlighten Americans about their character so they could use it wisely in their new world role.

In Mead's view, the most important influences on the national character were the geographic and social mobility of Americans and their diverse, immigrant pasts: "We are all third generation." Hungry for roots and a common identity, Americans turned away from but also imitated old-country traditions. They venerated the Republic's founders and myths. They shared memories by joining veterans' groups and expressing delight when a new acquaintance came from the same hometown or state; they sought a common ground in consumer brands (from Borden to Buick) and fraternal orders (from Elks to Kiwanis).

In moving around so much, Americans obscured most indicators of class, but they also ran into social groups whose rules of fair play they could not be sure of. Americans disapproved of bullying, or fighting for its own sake, but they also believed that people should be quick to stick up for themselves. The result was a defensive aggressiveness, especially among boys and men. Like many theorists of national character, Mead said little about differences of attitude between classes and the sexes; she had more to say, in fact, about Mom's influence on her sons than on her daughters.

For Mead, the key institution was the nuclear family, operating far from the guidance and support of older generations or extended kin. Parents, unsure deep down about what to aim for in raising their children, pressed them to achieve in the outside world, to attain more than the parents themselves had done but to do it in measurable and conventional ways: to hold their own in the playground, then get good grades, and later get good jobs. Without an uncle or a granny nearby, American children depended all the more on the love of their parents, who made it conditional on competitive but standardized achievement.[1]

In his introduction to *The American People,* the British anthropologist Geoffrey Gorer declared his debt to Margaret Mead as her student and colleague: he confessed he did not always know what ideas in his book were originally hers. Like Mead, he made much of the new American's wish to reject (or partially reject) the immigrant parent, but he focused this on the father. Antipaternalism was perpetuated by a primal myth of the Revolution, an Oedipal rejection of the European king. It fueled the traditional American hostility toward government, even to the point of lawless violence. At home, it reduced Dad's power to that of a big buddy, though his prowess at this or that might be boasted about around the block. Conversely, Mom's influence was expanded: she, and her symbols across the land, were seen as the fount of all good things, the cornucopia of liberty as well as the guardian of morality.

Gorer blamed on Mom Power much of the American male's fear of effeminacy and homosexuality. Pressured to be a 'he-man' and a 'regular guy,' he related more easily to hardware and machines than to people; friendships were extensive rather than deep. For both sexes, though, sissiness and passivity were off-limits from an early age. Gorer, like Mead, described American parents as an anxious lot, eager that their children should be 'independent,' that they should grow up, talk up, and measure up, engaging in play and competition with their peers.

Accepting Mead's theory that American parents made their love seem conditional on achievement, Gorer claimed that American children tended to be uncertain if they were achieving enough to earn that love. Hunger for love and attention led to a terror of being alone. The passion for joining clubs and fraternities, the rituals of dating, even the habit of leaving the radio on all day, were responses to the fear of being lonely and rejected. For Gorer, as for Mead, Americans valued individual assertion but only along rather narrow, heavily prescribed channels.[2]

Gorer and Mead were heirs to the spread of psychoanalytic writing in the 1920s and '30s. Some of their contemporaries reflected another prewar influence: the discussion of how American individualism could adapt to industrialization and the centralized modern state. The memory of New Deal politics and the wartime spectacle of the U.S. as a 'going concern' sharpened the interest.

The consensus of these studies was that Americans combined a buoyant, acquisitive individualism ('I can get it') with energetic co-operation ('We can do it') and a conformity to common goals and norms. In his massive book, *The American Democracy* (1949), the British socialist and political scientist Harold Laski declared that no other people had done so much to build "the idea of progress" into its "mental make-up." Along with this outlook went an impatient focus on the future rather than the past, a restless experimenting, and the idea that one was master of one's own fate.

Laski attributed these attitudes to the Revolution's break with "feudalism," and the pioneer's mastery of a great continent. This had helped to give a social, collective tinge to the nation's individualism. The national trait of expansiveness made Americans democratic and hospitable; and the faith in a boundless horizon for one's own advancement meant one believed in America as a land of special promise. Fulfilling that promise required efficient teamwork and a certain standardization—hence the tendency to dislike 'carping' eccentrics who did not show the national spirit. Laski also noted the traditional hostility to government, and a gap between the egalitarian aspect of American individualism and the forces of bigotry and economic "oligarchy."[3]

In another book of 1949, *Characteristically American,* the philosopher Ralph Barton Perry put even more stress on the competitive side of American individualism (both individual and team competition) and on the conforming and sociable side:

> The individual who holds himself apart, who will not "join," who does not "belong" . . . who does not "row his weight in the boat," is viewed with suspicion. Americans find silence hard to endure, and if they develop an oddity they make a fad of it so that they may dwell among similar oddities. Their individualism is a *collective* individualism—not the isolation of one human being, but the intercourse and cooperation of many.[4]

Neither Perry nor Laski, in the end, was very unhappy about conformism; both associated it with dynamic cooperation and a friendly and open gregariousness.

In 1950, there occurred the most significant event in the postwar history of American social-character studies—the publication of *The Lonely Crowd: A Study of the Changing American Character,* by David Riesman, in collaboration with two fellow sociologists, Nathan Glazer and Reuel Denney. *The Lonely Crowd* based its argument on the rise of a mass consumer society. It was also the first postwar book to make the psychology of conformity its main subject, and to detail a major shift in American character. So it was well in tune with the consumer boom after World War II, and the growing pervasiveness of brand-name products and look-alike suburbs.

A rich and complex work, *The Lonely Crowd* has been more cited, and more argued about, than any of its contemporaries and successors. Yet it heralded later findings to a degree that is seldom appreciated. Narcissism and "diffuse anxiety"; the shifting of authority from 'dos and don'ts' to manipulation and enticement; the flooding of attitudes by media messages; the channeling of achievement drives into competition for the approval of others; and the splintering of society into myriad interest groups—all these tendencies of modern American life that so worried commentators in the 1970s and '80s were spotted by Riesman et al. (and well before television had become an everyday staple).[5]

The Lonely Crowd set out three psychological "modes of conformity," corresponding to three stages in economic development. In highly stable, preindustrial societies, conformity tends to be "tradi-tion-directed," based on learning a detailed set of customs and prac-tices. By contrast, in societies whose populations and economies are expanding fast, the most suitable mode of conformity is "inner-di-rection." Detailed traditions will no longer do; instead the child in-ternalizes general precepts learned from elders at an early age. By adulthood, a person has acquired a fairly rigid morality and set of goals, which can, however, be adapted to new situations. In this kind of society, marked by heavy capital investment, much of work and life focuses on "the hardness of the material": on technical problems of production, and building and amassing *things*.

In the third stage of society, the major technical problems of pro-duction are solved. The culture shifts its concerns from production to consumption, and from a "psychology of scarcity" to a "psychology of abundance." Marketing and services develop; so does bureaucratic organization; and the art of working and living becomes one of relating to people rather than materials. Such conditions promote the rise of the "other-directed" character, equipped with sensitive anten-nae for peer-group tastes, shifting fashions, and media personalities. The inner-directed person might conform as much to public opinion but tended to want social *esteem*, whereas the other-directed person has a deeper need to be *liked* and to find resonance with others.

It is clear from Riesman's examples that he saw nineteenth-century America as prime soil for inner-direction (he did not say what char-acter mode he would assign to the colonial period). From the 1890s on, conditions were less promising for inner-direction, but Riesman believed that other-direction, as an American character type, had emerged only "in very recent years in the upper middle classes of our larger cities"—it was then percolating down the social structure. Since the new corporate economy, based on mass consumption, in-stallment buying, and fashion, was well established by the late 1920s—if somewhat interrupted by the Depression and World War II—Riesman's dating of American character shifts implies that eco-nomic change took time to work through into basic attitudes. Ries-man was not explicit about this; but he did say that the society still had many inner-directed, even tradition-directed, holdouts. Every-one, moreover, had elements of more than one type.

With his stress on general economic forces, Riesman resisted the 'exceptionalist' view, so common among writers of the 1940s, which attributed American character to a distinctive national history. He conjectured, indeed, that the maturing metropolitan civilizations of Athens and Rome had produced a lot of other-direction too. Still, Riesman vaguely conceded that American historical conditions, including the lack of "a seriously feudal past," made it easier for other-direction to take root (lack of 'feudalism' presumably encouraged sensitivity to a changing public opinion), and he identified America's urban upper-income youth as world leaders of the modern trend. I might add that the idea of a "psychology of abundance" was at its most plausible before the early 1970s, when the energy crisis and foreign cost-competition warned Americans that technical problems of production were still crucial.

Riesman traced the formation of his character types in child-rearing and in adult life at work and play. In conditions of inner-direction, parents were strict and demanding, but the home provided more psychological privacy than it did later, when families became smaller and more emotional attention was paid to each child. In conditions of other-direction, the child becomes more self-conscious of relationships with others. Parents are less sure of their authority and share more of it with the media and the children's contemporaries. Teachers develop the skills of getting on with others rather than 'hard' content; consumption itself is valued as sociable experience. As the peer group becomes more important, the child or youth tries to impress others in marginal aspects of taste and style (rather like a brand product) but has no wish to stand out as a big and forceful hero. Riesman's picture of the modern young American has less open aggression in it than the character described by Mead, Gorer, and other writers of the forties.

In adult life, Riesman's middle-class American uses fun at work (the office party, the expense-account lunch) and works at having fun outside the office. This idea of a mutual invasion of work and play puts *The Lonely Crowd* midway between Margaret Mead's stress on achievement drives and the hedonism portrayed by writers in the late seventies and early eighties.

Riesman admitted ruefully that his picture of other-direction was a lot more unattractive to Americans than his portrait of inner-direction: the new type looked shallow and manipulative; the old one stern and strong if moralistic. Riesman himself did not agree with this preference for the old type. He believed that other-directed people tended to be more tolerant and humane; their defects were simply more contemporary than those of the inner-directed, who conformed just as much to external requirements. His own ideal was another type, the *autonomous* person.

Riesman's autonomous character was less deeply embedded than the other types in a social and economic system; it was freer "to choose whether to conform or not." Although Riesman did not say so, it is clear that the age of inner-direction, as he portrayed it, gave more scope for autonomy than the age of other-direction. In the earlier period, when authority was clear-cut and less insidious, and spheres of work and play were more sharply separated, it was easier to rebel or hide away.

Riesman's ideal of autonomy showed that he was more concerned at that time with the costs of overconformity than with the danger of selfishness and isolation. Despite his book's title, he touched but briefly on the subject of loneliness. In different ways it characterized both the inner-directed and other-directed, but the other-directed, Riesman implied, were more afraid of it. Beneath his adept fielding of social cues, the other-directed person remained "a lonely member of the crowd because he never (came) really close to the others or himself." Riesman suggested, rather enigmatically, that Americans would only find a real "neighborhood" of social bonds when they paid more attention to their own thoughts and feelings and lives.[6]

In the 'Eisenhower fifties,' a number of survey researchers gave bad marks to college students for being politically passive and obsessed with economic security. Some commentators attributed this to the Depression traumas of their parents; others, to McCarthyism. When the *Fortune* writer William Whyte published *The Organization Man* in 1956, his findings resonated with these comments, and his title coined a term.[7]

Unlike David Riesman, Whyte claimed that middle-class Americans had become *more* conformist. Led by the young adult generation, they had shifted from a "Protestant Ethic" of self-reliance—the "pursuit of individual salvation through hard work, thrift, and competitive struggle"—to a "Social Ethic," which endorsed the "pressures of society against the individual." While older leaders sincerely hailed the Protestant Ethic as the ark of American achievement, more and more people believed that *belonging* to an organized group was the "ultimate need of the individual," and that creativity came not from the individual but from the group—the committee, the research team.

The business corporation, archetype of the new collective, took care of the executive employee's welfare, encouraging consumption as well as hardworking loyalty. The result was some ambivalence about the claims of work versus leisure, office versus home. Competitiveness went into climbing the corporate ladder; few people thought big or bucked the collective standards. Few indeed wanted to, for the organization enlisted the social sciences to present the goals and values of the group as scientific, value-free propositions. Any conflict between individual and organization, or between a class of employees and top management, was merely a problem of communication and personal adjustment, a matter for 'human relations' experts and the personnel department.

Whyte wrote mainly about male businessmen and professionals (he had nothing on professional women), but he did devote several chapters to life among the garden apartments of Park Forest, a Chicago suburb especially designed for married professionals with small children. Although Park Forest was unusually communal, Whyte found significance in it as a township of "transients." The young mothers and fathers of Park Forest were sociable and outgoing, active in local associations. They suppressed their needs for privacy and differentness, but they also held back from deep attachments to their neighbors, for soon they would be moving on to new locations and assignments. As David Riesman said of his other-directed characters, they were "at home everywhere and nowhere"—not rootless but like plants whose roots were shallow and many.

Whyte's older, Protestant Ethic type was quite similar to Riesman's inner-directed character. His view of what caused its decline was like Riesman's but narrower. The main cause, for Whyte, was the rise of bureaucratic organization at the turn of the century, reinforced by Progressive attacks on laissez-faire economics. All this, however, had taken time to work through to basic attitudes. These factors, Whyte recognized, were not peculiar to the U.S., but they had a special poignancy for Americans because of the nation's traditional belief in individualism.

Whyte himself believed the "Social Ethic" to be lopsided, stultifying, and subtly oppressive. In attacking it he wanted to go back, not to robber-baron individualism but to that precarious American mixture of self-reliance and cooperation which had struck Alexis de Tocqueville in the 1830s. Whyte insisted that he had no quarrel with the "surface uniformities of American life," with "ranch wagons, or television sets, or gray flannel suits." He doubted, indeed, that Americans, on this level, had become more conformist. On a deeper level, though, he believed they had: they were more dependent psychologically on the organized group.

In the early 1960s, three essays by the historian David Potter partially reversed Whyte's historical sequence. Potter agreed that Americans had moved away from an ethic of self-reliance—if tough guys and compulsive winners still flourished, they did so more defensively. But he also believed that this shift was a move away from conformity.

In "The Quest for the National Character" (1962), Potter distinguished two egalitarian traditions in America: the belief in equal opportunity to win unequal rewards, and the insistence that all people shared a common humanity and basic rights to individual dignity. The first tradition, best suited to a "new, undeveloped frontier country," stressed a competitive self-reliance in seeking material success. The second tradition was antiauthoritarian; it tabooed snobbish airs and overbearing behavior; it encouraged leadership by signals and persuasion rather than command. If it produced independence of mind, it also produced its opposite, submissiveness to majority opinion.

Potter's follow-up essay, "American Individualism in the Twentieth Century" (1963), adjusted these distinctions to a statement of historical change. American preferences, he believed, had shifted from one kind of individualism to another. Influenced perhaps by the liberal movements of the late fifties and early sixties, he claimed that twentieth-century Americans had come to value *individuality*: nonconformity, self-expression, and dissent. Their nineteenth-century predecessors were more apt to associate individualism with practical *self-reliance*; and the narrow frontier and business life that demanded self-reliance in economic matters also promoted cultural conformity. The fact that dissent and nonconformity possessed their own, long American tradition, and the converse fact that modern dissenters often conformed to their own groups, only modified the general shift.

In the case of women, Potter had already outlined a similar, but not identical, change—a claim that worked against Riesman's historical thesis. In "American Women and the American Character" (1962), he suggested that their traditional dependence had long made them other-directed ("sensitive to the moods and interests of others"), even if they had also been inner-directed in defending the values of the home. They now had more choice and independence than before, but they were also under more pressure to fill a multiplicity of roles. Although modern society gave women more chance to work outside the home (usually in low-paid jobs), it still expected them to be domestic managers and buyers, subject to the demeaning tricks of male advertisers. Impelled by American traditions to be more assertive than their European counterparts, they were nonetheless indoctrinated against challenging men. The American woman, as a result, "still [hesitated] to claim individualism as a quality of her own."

Both of Potter's main types of individualism—self-reliance and individuality—were supposed, in his reading of American values, to serve "group welfare." American democracy had never exalted "man in isolation," still less the kind of hauteur that flouted popular convention. Although Potter recognized that American individualism— both old and new—could be antisocial, the atomizing of America by unlimited individualism was not seen as a problem in these essays.[8]

Some years before, Potter had begun to acknowledge just such a problem, though hope took the edge off his anxiety. In *People of Plenty: Economic Abundance and the American Character* (1954), Potter claimed that abundance was the main cause of that character's distinctive qualities. Unlike Riesman, he did not see this as just a modern force; it had operated through most, if not all, of the nation's history. American abundance came from an interaction between rich natural resources and organized technology, and the latter in turn required certain habits of mind. Potter said little about the original source and nature of these attitudes, except to venture that, from the eighteenth century on, "Anglo-Americans [unlike the Spanish] were particularly apt at exploiting the new country."

In Potter's view, many of the American traits attributed by Frederick Jackson Turner to the frontier were in fact the result of abundance. They resulted, that is, from the 'free land' aspect of the frontier, and from urban, industrial abundance, which continued after the frontier had 'closed.' Potter quotes, in this context, one of Turner's classic statements:

That coarseness and strength combined with acuteness and inquis-
itiveness; that practical, inventive turn of mind, quick to find ex-
pedients; that masterful grasp of material things, lacking in the
artistic but powerful to effect great ends; that restless, nervous
energy; that dominant individualism, working for good and for evil,
and withal that buoyancy and exuberance which comes with
freedom—these are the traits of the frontier, or traits called out
elsewhere because of the existence of the frontier.[9]

Potter did not actually say if he connected all these traits with
abundance itself. Certainly he recognized special influences on American character in the frontier experience. By accepting hardship now
in return for prosperity later, he suggested, the pioneer had to be an
optimist, a believer in progress. Likewise, the settler's isolated, self-
sufficient way of life made him an individualist. On the other hand,
American inventiveness and readiness to try something new stemmed
mainly from a fast-growing and changing technology, "far away from
the frontier."

Potter also contended that abundance supported democratic attitudes; it enabled almost everyone to have high expectations and feel
qualified to have a say in government. Abundance, for Potter, meant
widely distributed abundance, and with that went mass education.
Potter's Americans also assumed abundance to be continually ex-
pandable: wealth did not have to be redistributed for everyone to get
more.

It was on just this point, the matter of expectations, that Potter saw
the main problem for his people of plenty. Expanding abundance
helped people move around and move up, to the point where class
barriers to advancement seemed illegitimate; but the ideal of mobility
for all caused frustration and insecurity when people still bumped up
against social barriers. It also deprived people of true *status,* the sense
of worth that comes from belonging to any class that is defined by and
respected for the work it does. The machine destruction of craftwork
added to these injuries.

In cautious hope, however, Potter declared that contemporary
abundance was so great and so spread about that the economy no
longer needed mobility as an engine of development, and individuals
no longer needed it to be prosperous. As life ceased to be a compul-
sory race for scarce goods, there was less hierarchy about, and com-

panies and unions were trying to give employees a new sense of secure membership in the organization. What William Whyte saw as a pernicious cult of belonging, Potter saw as a road to psychological health.

Whereas Potter dealt with status and conformity in separate writings, the two were put together in a wide-ranging interpretation by the political sociologist Seymour Martin Lipset in 1963. Lipset's essay "A Changing American Character?" explicitly rebutted the claim by Riesman and Whyte that changing economic conditions were transforming the people. The strongest influence on their character was, he believed, a traditional culture of achievement and equality.

Because of these two values, what was distinctive about American character had not changed since the early nineteenth century; their source lay in the "interplay" between Puritanism and a "Revolutionary ethos," unrestricted by a "feudal past." Achievement and equality met in the idea of equal *opportunity* to do well, but a tension remained between the egalitarian tendency to friendliness and generosity and the special snobberies that came from trying to achieve status in a society where class distinctions were unclear and insecure. Conforming to a status group, however, was compatible with learning social skills for success: getting ahead by getting along.

Lipset conceded that modern factors—bureaucracy, urbanization, and the growth of services—had made Americans more sensitive to the "judgment of others." Compared with the European model, however, American conformity to opinion was not new. It had been observed by foreign travelers at many points in the nineteenth century, and it resulted from egalitarianism as much as from status ambition.

Lipset did not believe that bureaucracy had reduced competitive drive and achievement at work. On the contrary, the organization man's other-direction kept him working hard in response to group pressures; the prospect of promotion was an effective substitute for the incentives of ownership. Meanwhile, other developments, including the growth of education, were providing more scope for artistic and intellectual individuality; and the very acceptance of outward conventions could release "psychic energy" for private self-fulfillment. Lipset's American character combined some of the conformity stressed by writers in the 1950s with the drive for self-fulfillment that writers of the 1970s and '80s would make much more of. For Lipset, the constants in American character, its traditional mix of conformity and individualism, enabled it to adapt both to modern organization and to new opportunities for self-expression.[10]

Lipset's essay ended in a swell of optimism: Americans were showing that they could get together productively while being themselves. Two other writers responded in different ways to America's dynamic economy of the 1950s and the early '60s. The historian George Pierson and the anthropologist Jules Henry were far apart in approach and tone, yet both raised questions about the *affiliativeness* of Americans.[11]

In four articles (dated 1954 and 1962–64), Pierson claimed that movement itself was the key to American character. No single cause "made and kept us different," but the main one was the "M-factor": movement, migration, mobility. The M-factor included colonial settlement, immigration, upward mobility, and all the moving about that Americans did so much of, to cities as well as to the wilderness. It had called out specific classes and personalities to the New World and to western opportunity; but movement was effect as well as cause. *"L'inquiétude du caractère"*—the restless temper—that Tocqueville had noted in 1831 was still a distinctive American tendency in the 1960s.[12]

The M-factor accented youthful vigor, bustle, and the optimism of the "up and coming," though it also gave new space to conservatives fleeing change: indeed, it accommodated extremes of political temperament. At the same time, it often encouraged an informal, egalitarian mixing, taking people 'as they come.' It promoted 'joining,' not just for neighborly help in new places but to ward off loneliness. Americans were truly a "lonely crowd, restless, detached and craving of company."

Pierson sprinkled his pieces with vivid examples and quotations; he wrote in a chatty, exuberant style well suited to his subject. Implicitly he enjoyed the great American "Freedom to Move" (1963). Over the years, however, he let the shadows lengthen. His article of 1954 concluded that Americans had adjusted well to their instability, but it began by explaining to foreigners the disturbing contradictions of a great power. Influenced perhaps by the spectacle of McCarthyism, he attributed the country's moralistic laws and the people's fear of public opinion to the insecurities of a moving populace.

More than this: If movement had made America the "land of the second chance," that chance often meant ducking obligations and escaping a seamy past. By 1963, as liberals rediscovered the poor, Pierson was applying his ideas about escape to the urban slum, deserted by its more successful and mobile inhabitants. He also wrote of the destruction wrought by mobile Americans on the environment, and the "dreary monotony" of nuclear-family homes spread without much community across a "once-smiling nature." America long had been, still was, a nation of friendly, outgoing strangers, cooperative but not rooted in particular places or each other. Like David Riesman and William Whyte, but more so, Pierson portrayed a people that was sociable rather than intimate. For most mobile Americans, indeed, their "wandering star" was "baleful and ultimately destructive" of nature and of civilization.[13]

George Pierson expressed reservations about American culture; Jules Henry scourged it. His book *Culture Against Man* (1963) was the first account of American character to include Cold War attitudes and, more briefly, the fear of nuclear annihilation. It also paid more attention to class differences and to working-class conditions than did most American character studies. While following David Riesman in stressing the psychology of consumption, it made more distinction than he did between a consumer "pseudo-self," imposed on the individual by an economic system (especially advertising), and the values of a truer, deeper self. It reflected here the concern about advertising power that had made such a market for Vance Packard's book of 1957, *The Hidden Persuaders*. Although it said little about the structure of that power, it was an indirect response to a trend long identified by economists: the growing domination of industry and marketing by relatively few, giant firms.[14]

Like so many theorists of American character, Henry began with a selective reference to the great French count. Americans, he said, still exhibited that lonely independence and grim, feverish drive for acquisition and self-improvement which Tocqueville had observed in the 1830s. The opportunity presented to early immigrants on a boundless continent had fostered "insatiability" and "drivenness." The uncertainties born of technological change had inflamed these attitudes, and the modern economic system had rechanneled them. "Drivenness" and competitiveness at work were now concentrated within the executive and professional class. Other people had become passive and security-minded, for their work was at once routine and insecure, threatened by "human obsolescence" through new technology.

In all classes, however, the old trait of insatiability appeared in the drive to acquire and enjoy more consumer goods. At the same time, the advertising industry and the Cold War combined to produce "acquiescence." Mentally softened by the pseudologic and pseudorealities of advertising, Americans accepted Cold War dogmas and projected their competitive fears onto the world.

Henry distinguished economic, expansionist drives, at work and in consumption, from "values" of kindness, love, and gentleness. People deep down felt these to be the real virtues but confined them mainly to home life. The cause of this tension lay in the economic system. It amounted to a race between producing more and consuming more. For most people, even the system's elite engineers, work was dull and narrow, providing no space for community. Americans compensated by consuming, grimly seeking escape in fun and thereby eroding the "impulse-control" that hard work needed.

At home, fathers dumped their work frustrations on the family; they tried to be old-fashioned disciplinarians, but they also wanted to be chums with their children, abetting and imitating their consumption. America's youth were no exception to this general picture of misery. In neighborhoods where families came and went, young people had to work hard at making friends. They competed so much for popularity and felt so self-conscious about it that they found it difficult to form close and trusting friendships.

In line with Jules Henry, a growing number of commentators from the late 1950s on realized that bureaucracy and consumer conformity did not necessarily mean community: what robbed the self might also starve social relationships. The American fear that materialism would undermine human and spiritual relationships was older than the Republic, but it acquired new force in the 1960s when hippies and radicals attacked the 'plastic' relationships of suburban and corporate life. (What bankers' gold was to the agrarian Populists and 'silverites' of the 1880s and '90s, plastic was to the 1960s 'counterculture.') If you were 'in touch with' yourself and nature, if you expressed yourself spontaneously, unobstructed by assigned roles and elaborate acquisitions, you would have closer, more open relations with others. Competitiveness and the urge to dominate were artificial traits, imposed by the business corporation and the 'technocratic' state.

The book on social character that most fully expressed this view was written not by an occupational hippie but by a Yale law professor! Charles Reich's *The Greening of America* (1970) divided American character into three types of "consciousness." The chief representatives of "Consciousness I" were small businessmen and farmers, the heirs to early republican and frontier individualism. Their forebears had pursued genuine self-fulfillment in a spirit of sharing and equality; but usually they had repressed and narrowed themselves, and now their individualism had shriveled them. Mean-minded and grasping, they disliked big organization but could not comprehend its ramifications.[15]

"Consciousness II" commanded the people of that organization: professionals; classifiers; practitioners of hierarchy, rational order, and the denial of wonderment. Consciousness II had started in liberal reforms aimed to control 'robber baron' individualism, but its functionaries had become the manipulators of a "false consciousness": they served the system by imposing its artificial values on themselves and others, and suppressing true sensibility.

"Consciousness III" carried Reich's hopes for America. As yet, he admitted, it was confined almost entirely to a segment of youth, a generation freed from old pressures and constraints by modern affluence and technology; though it also drew on Afro culture and on sensitive spirits going back to Whitman and Thoreau. The modern flowering of Consciousness III came from the disjunction between the full life touted by modern organization and the desolation it had perpetrated: "war upon nature," "neon ugliness," dehumanized jobs, violence in Vietnam. Reich did not reject technology per se; he would have it used for genuine liberation. Consciousness III, he insisted, started with "the self" as "the only true reality," but that reality did not include selfishness. Consciousness III was open to new experience, honest and giving to others, forever in a "state of becoming." For Reich, protean individualism would not unravel America; it would join it.

In 1970, the year *The Greening of America* was published, a harsher book on American character also appeared, an angry response to the violence and racial conflicts of the sixties and the U.S. bombing and shelling of the Vietnamese countryside. *The Pursuit of Loneliness: American Culture at the Breaking Point,* by the sociologist Philip Slater, made no mention of the famed American friendliness.

Instead Slater found on returning from abroad a "grim monotony" in American faces—"hard, surly, and bitter," with an "aura of deprivation."

Slater's book was an all-out, psychological attack on American individualism, past as well as present. Where Whyte, Pierson, and Henry had found a shallow sociability, Slater saw a profounder isolation of the individual (or individual family). And whereas Reich's most urgent agenda was the development of self, from which a true community would emerge, Slater put things the other way about. When Americans had established truer, deeper relations with others, they would realize themselves as individuals.[16]

As a radical of the 1960s, Slater considered Americans to have a repressive social character. He implied that this explained their 'backlash' against poverty programs and political protest. In Slater's view, America's competitive individualism frustrated basic human desires for community, interdependence, and engagement with social reality—involvement, that is, with the real issues and problems that existed around them. To suppress their social yearning, Americans had to be all the more hostile to collectivist radicals, who reminded them of what they could be.

Slater's thesis implied that Riesman's nineteenth-century inner-directed type was still very much around. Slater believed that a mobile, individualist middle class kept itself in order by depending heavily on self-control. This impelled Americans to suppress feelings and spontaneity; to resent and fear deviants who stood for emotional freedom; and to load the care of 'difficult' people upon technical devices (police cars and asylums) rather than upon the community as a whole. The paradox was that if people would only recognize their dependence on others and on authority, and rely less on self-control (the anxious cop inside them), they would let themselves be more tolerant of individual differences and self-expression.

Slater attributed American pathology to two main causes, aside from individualism itself. First, he believed like George Pierson that the much-vaunted migration and movement of Americans selected people who were inclined to escape problems rather than confront them. Second, Americans had used technology to insulate themselves from others and from social problems in highly equipped private homes. In pursuit of an arid self-sufficiency, Americans made many of their outside contacts into irksome experiences to be got through as quickly as possible, from shopping in the supermarket to driving on the freeway.

At home, men treated women as an "opiate" against the aggressive social system outside. Parents pushed children to deny their needs for dependence and interdependence; if this pressure had abated in recent years, it still deprived children of the support they needed from parents amid the flux of modern society. Parents now let their children go after success in a wider range of fields than before, but they still overloaded them with their own frustrated ambitions. Not knowing if they were measuring up, the children often became hungry for attention and narcissistic. This effect was much as Geoffrey Gorer had described it, but the behavior that came out of it was less sociable.

In Slater's view, Americans had been cursed from the start, from the earliest impact of migration and mobility; but modern technology had made matters worse by expanding violence while encouraging retreat. The disappearance of old communities, "oases" of noncompetitiveness such as neighborhoods and extended families, drove people to find affection and easy-going acceptance in ersatz forms, from popular lyrics to film comedies. As Americans isolated themselves in their homes and equipment, while letting their aggressiveness play on the larger society, so their fears mounted.

Slater did find some hope in the new cultural and political movements of the 1960s, but he was more conscious than Reich of their flaws and contradictions. He liked the communal egalitarianism, but he thought that the hippie ethic of 'doing your own thing' was just another form of an old and selfish American individualism.

With the exception of Philip Slater and Charles Reich, practically no one wrote about modern American character as such between the mid-1960s and mid-'70s. The lull was due to the centrifugal vision of the 1960s, the value placed on appreciating the distinctive lives of minorities and the underprivileged—blacks, women, the poor. The intellectual revolt against 'consensus history' (which was largely white, middle- and upper-class, male history) moved the study of American culture away from generalizing about national character into the discovery of subcultures, producing reports and stories with a 'sense of place.'

These new concerns shaped the interpretation of American character when that enterprise was revived in the late seventies. Examining local communities and working-class culture in the eighteenth and nineteenth centuries, social historians often found the bogeyman in nascent market capitalism, commercializing and rupturing the human ties and rich relationships of local life. At the same time, there was discussion about 'mentalité' in early America and the emergence of an 'entrepreneurial personality' type. This moved some historians back toward concepts of social character.[17]

For the more left-wing historians and sociologists, the divisive and selfish side of capitalism seemed especially relevant amid the fiscal conservatism of the seventies, when 'stagflation' encouraged all Presidents of the decade—Carter as well as the Republicans—to curb domestic government spending, including welfare budgets. In 1978, *The Culture of Inequality,* by the sociologist Michael Lewis, criticized the "individual-as-central" ethos of Americans, not just for attributing poverty to the poor themselves (either to their moral defects or to their social-psychological inadequacies) but for *requiring* the existence of a poor class in order to salvage the egos of the nonpoor.

According to Lewis, the belief in open opportunity to reach the top meant that many people throughout the society felt they had failed. To compensate, they sought "counterfeit" success in the achievement of their children, in "symbolic consumption" (from big cars to ornamental chess sets), and in positions and titles in associations (from Rotary vice-president to Loyal Knight of the Elks). These compensations, however, were not enough, so it helped to have a visible class of real 'failures,' the poor, to convince the others of their solid, hardworking achievement.[18]

By the late 1970s, a number of commentators were remarking on what seemed to be a new selfishness in American life. On the left, the fault was attributed to consumer capitalism; on the right, to the 'permissive society,' evidenced in ever-mounting divorces and the 'breakup' of families. For observers of many persuasions, the dissipation of the 1960s 'counterculture' into 'expressive lifestyles' supplied awesome exhibits of what Tom Wolfe had called the "Me Decade." In fact the showy hedonists and spiritual self-seekers that Wolfe and others wrote about were concentrated in college towns and the more stylish city sections; but this was just where America's cultural pundits tended to live or work—including Christopher Lasch (University of Rochester, New York).[19]

Lasch's book of 1979, *The Culture of Narcissism: American Life in an Age of Diminishing Expectations,* put together an indictment of capitalism and modern mass organization with a defense of the traditional family and a qualified respect for old individualist disciplines. Capitalism had "severed the ties of personal dependence only to revive dependence under cover of bureaucratic rationality"; by surrounding the individual with a net of public relations and pseudo-smiles, it had undermined "patriarchy"—the tough, moral leadership of fathers and father-figures. Modern organization (government as well as business) had taken away people's sense of personal, moral responsibility without providing a clear authority of its own. It encouraged manipulative warfare between individuals while massaging them with commodities, packaged experience, and media fantasies. The result was a personality that felt empty, isolated, and vaguely vengeful.[20]

As Lasch read American history, prevailing notions of self-improvement in the eighteenth and nineteenth centuries had all been associated with achieving something real and lasting: clearing a farm, opening a store, endowing a library. With the rise of modern organization, however, capitalist individualism had turned in on itself. In a vortex between the organized "cult of consumption" and fears of economic and global catastrophe, "immediate gratification" replaced long-term goals. Success in the organization merely meant getting good publicity and beating out others by presenting "winning images" of oneself. Lasch indeed asserted that Americans had become *more* competitive in the twentieth century, while depending on others for recognition and goodies.

As Lasch noted, much of this historical shift resembled the changes described by Riesman, Whyte, and others, but beneath the modern norm of 'getting along' he saw a different person, a character type that was more ambitiously aggressive and self-centered. Without truly binding the individual, mass organization had taken over and distorted his or her sense of reality through its array of media instruments, from advertising and managed news to television shows and videos. Information was increasingly secondhand and prerecorded. Society had become a "hall of mirrors" in which fictions mocked other fictions ('soaps' spoofing other 'soaps'), leaving to individual dignity only a sense of ironic detachment. While cynically escaping into fantasy from the degrading routines of modern work, people lost a clear sense of truth and untruth, and of self in relation to others.

Just as the synthetic reality of the media had invaded the self, so the professional propaganda of child-rearing—put out by counselors, progressive teachers, and advice-book writers—had invaded the family. Even when the current fad told parents to 'act out' their feelings, parents followed the advice too anxiously to behave naturally to their children. This applied particularly to mothers, who often felt they had to make up for the absence of the father. Eager to be loving and encouraging, but really wrapped up in themselves, parents conveyed an underlying coolness to their children, who in turn became insecure narcissists: self-aggrandizing (in subtle ways), hungry for admiration, yet emotionally passive and resistant to intimacy.

The 'awareness movement' of the late sixties and the seventies was no antidote to these trends; on the contrary, it had moved from trivializing political protest by vaunting it as *experience* to abandoning politics altogether in private self-obsessions. These impoverished the individual by blocking out society.

Throughout his complex argument, Lasch stressed the effect of existential terror. The fear of annihilation, sharpened by the Jewish Holocaust and nuclear weapons, was magnified by the media's swiftness to report violence and disaster, from murders and plane crashes to famines and earthquakes. To this was added economic and ecological worries (here Lasch was clearly influenced by America's new economic pessimism of the 1970s). These fears made people live for themselves in the present. They lost a sense of community, not just with contemporaries but with the past and the future.

In Lasch's view of history, the basic change in social character wrought by capitalism was a very long-term business—a matter of centuries rather than decades. Even the engines of annihilation and damage to the environment could be seen as products of industrial organization, though Lasch did not explicitly connect them to capitalism per se.

In 1980, a reappraisal of the national character by David Riesman concurred that Americans had become more selfish, but unlike Lasch, and unlike his own book of 1950 (*The Lonely Crowd*), it found the main cause in developments since World War II. Riesman's essay "Egocentrism: Is the American Character Changing?" pointed out that egoism itself was not new: viz., the "imperial self" of some nineteenth-century romantics and entrepreneurs, and the narcissism of various leaders throughout American history. What was new was "public approval" of openly "self-serving conduct." The 1960s cult of candor and openness ('let it all hang out') had made hypocrisy a worse offense than egoism, which was now peddled as therapy. The result was a snowballing effect, as more and more people assumed that everyone else was 'looking out for number one' and acted accordingly.

Riesman cited studies of college students, which indicated that cheating and inconsiderate behavior had grown over the previous few decades. This was partly due, he believed, to the crowding of campuses by the 'baby boom' generation, which had heightened student competition and pressured faculties and deans to defer to youth. Widespread affluence, moreover, had protracted adolescence into the thirties and even the forties, producing "pseudo-youths" who refused long-term commitments. Riesman agreed with Lasch that a consumer, throwaway attitude to feelings and relationships diminished people's involvement in the world. The idea that all experience, however transitory, was equal and could be obtained without deep investment merely flattened and reduced a person's emotional life.[21]

In Riesman's view, a growth in egalitarianism since World War II had bestowed more recognition on minorities and underdog groups. This had raised expectations, and so had the expansion of college education. More and more people now wanted the perks and the glitter—"dramatic gratifications"—displayed in the national media, which in turn tended to ignore the very different values and styles of old-fashioned, local communities. In complex ways too, feminism and the Pill encouraged parents to focus on their own lives and ambitions without feeling they had to make as many sacrifices for their children, or indeed for each other.

Looking back toward his earlier writing, Riesman believed that the 1950s concern with conformity, stimulated by the rise of "corporate civil servants" to the top of business, had produced a wrongheaded reaction. In seeking to restore a lost American individualism, people often forgot that Tocqueville's individualists had to have self-control because of economic scarcity (Riesman's view again differed from David Potter's theory of early abundance). Tocqueville's Americans were also keen participants in voluntary associations. In modern times, by contrast, erosion of ethnic ties had removed a major source of social and political action.

Riesman recognized "a strong intellectual counterattack . . . now under way against the encroachments of egocentrism." He noted the proposals for reviving neighborhood communities, sometimes on an ethnic basis, and he believed that more students were getting involved in political causes and social service. Academically, he praised those college administrations that were trying to combat the "over-optioned life" with a more rigorous and cohesive curriculum. In society at large, however, much more had to be done to foster that "diligent cooperation," that sense of interdependence, so urgently needed to control the technology of 'Spaceship Earth.'

In 1981, the year after Riesman's reappraisal, there appeared the first book on American character by an opinion pollster. Daniel Yankelovich's account, sonorously titled *New Rules: Searching for Self-Fulfillment in a World Turned Upside Down,* combined statistics with flesh and blood. From his interview files he gave vignettes of individual men and women, working class as well as middle class. Yankelovich agreed with Lasch that "pre-occupation with self [was] a sign of the times," but he vehemently denied that narcissistic personality structures lay at the heart of it. Although he criticized much of what he found, his tone was sympathetic, and he was ultimately sanguine that the ethic of self-fulfillment could be redeemed and redirected.[22]

Relying as he did on recent survey research, Yankelovich took a shorter-term view than Lasch. As he saw it, the widespread concern with psychological self-fulfillment came out of the enormous growth in the consumer economy following World War II. Not until the seventies, however, did the demand for self-fulfillment extend much beyond a campus minority. The turning point came in the 1960s, when a new generation, not raised on scarcity, abandoned the "giving/getting covenant" that had governed their parents' lives. Under this compact, people made sacrifices for an improved standard of living in the future and a decent home and family. In varying degrees, the new generation rejected the self-denial implied by this; one might not be exactly rich, but the economy would go on growing. It would deliver security and wider opportunities for most people, including women and minorities.

Yet the new generation built on (or, rather, infilled) their parents' half-suppressed dreams of the good life. Definitions of that life turned inward, moving beyond material consumption to psychological richness and the freedom to express one's own identity. By the late 1970s, "millions of Americans [were] hungry to live their lives to the brim, determined to consume every dish on the smorgasbord of human experience." Work had moved off center stage. Doing good and satisfying work was still valued, but fewer people assumed that effort per se paid off. Manual workers as well as professionals were now more critical of their jobs, judging them by standards of self-fulfillment.

Yankelovich found much to commend in these standards. They represented, he believed, a search for a "new American philosophy of life." They accompanied a 'live and let live' tolerance. They could be tapped by efforts to make work more civilized and more productive. And in times of economic stringency, they might serve Americans better than the old insistence on outsize consumption (the big tail-fin car of the 1950s). Yankelovich, nonetheless, believed that the quest for self-fulfillment had taken a wrong turn. For one thing, the quest was economically vulnerable. It still assumed a considerable economic backup, to make it possible, for instance, to buy a more 'expressive' apartment or get a more satisfying but less secure job. *New Rules* describes people who got overextended in this way in the 1970s when the economy leveled out and inflation went up.

Psychologically, too, the quest for self-fulfillment was flawed. Intense focus on the self was not only selfish but self-starving, since it cut off the individual from social issues and involvement. (Yankelovich's position here was much like that of Riesman, Lasch, and Slater.) In addition, the theories of A. A. Maslow and others celebrating "self-actualization" presented desires as a progression of "needs," which one *ought* to satisfy. This put people into two kinds of stress. First, it caused conflicts of feelings and relationships—the misery, for example, when a couple tried to be open and 'emancipated' about having other sexual partners. Second, when self-fulfillment became a moral imperative ('I owe it to myself'), the sheer job of satisfying diverse 'needs' became a burden. Yankelovich quoted a woman in therapy at a dazzling moment of truth: "You mean I don't have to do what I want to do?"

Writing around the time of Ronald Reagan's election in 1980, Yankelovich had to recognize right-wing reactions against permissive self-fulfillment, but he made more of other responses. Rejecting the 'pendulum' theory that Americans would simply return to old values, he believed he saw the beginnings of a new awareness that the truest self-fulfillment came through commitment to others and a sense of relationship to the past, the future, and the natural environment. In his own surveys, a growing number of people said they were trying to satisfy a need for community based on shared interests or backgrounds. The proportion of adult Americans acknowledging this had risen from about a third in the early seventies to nearly half by 1980.

Four years after *New Rules* was published, the sociologist of religion Robert Bellah and four other sociologists and social philosophers returned the discussion of American individualism to a longer-term historical analysis. As if to counteract the unsocial tendencies they found, their book, *Habits of the Heart: Individualism and Commitment in American Life* (1985), was a sprawling team effort—flabby in places, acute in others. It concentrated on a number of middle-class communities and individuals in California and the Northeast.[23]

Like Yankelovich, Bellah and company found differing mixtures of individualism and civic spirit, but they claimed, rather vaguely, that Americans lacked an effective and rich *language* of community. Americans were often afraid of talking about the community they really wanted, lest it diminish the independence they traditionally valued. Their difficulty in forming a more cooperative philosophy stemmed in part from the eclipse of colonial Puritan and early republican traditions. Both traditions had combined their own types of individualism with a sense of obligation to others and to common institutions. Their influence had survived into the present, but two other traditions had shaped modern American character more powerfully. The first was "utilitarian individualism": Calculate your interest, work hard to improve and raise yourself, and success would be yours. It was personified in the eighteenth century by Benjamin Franklin.

The second of the two more modern traditions, "expressive individualism," started in the early nineteenth century as a reaction against the first. Stressing love, feelings, and the deepest expression of self, it was personified by Walt Whitman. In their early forms, both traditions made a place for citizenship and social bonds, but these values waned as the economy waxed; Americans came to expect that individualism would automatically expand the GNP and nourish the culture.

As the authors saw it, however, utilitarian individualism in the twentieth century often assumed a bureaucratic form: climbing the ladder. The authors took a much dimmer view of this than Seymour Martin Lipset had (see page 24). Promotion, not work itself, had become important, yet this did not stop people from feeling engulfed by organization. Meanwhile, utilitarian and expressive individualism converged in the *therapeutic relationship,* which became a model for many relationships in a society where more and more people managed other people or provided services. In the therapeutic relationship, two people communicate intensely without *doing* much together. They relate on unequal terms for particular payoffs (a fee or professional satisfaction for the therapist; health or relief for the client). Moral commitments to a given community or value system yield to the question: What works best for you?

Despite the ministrations of therapy, the authors—like Jules Henry—found an excessive divide in American life between the private world of love and reflection and the public world of competitive striving. Some people did bridge the two, infusing their public life with moral meaning and caring for others. Even those who embarked on intense voyages of self-discovery sometimes found that their ships were social vessels: other people were on board. In general, though, American life was too fragmented and specialized to encourage a wide civic vision. Even when consumption was enjoyed in the company of others, it was usually practiced in "lifestyle enclaves."

On this last point Bellah et al. slid from decrying a *lack* of community to criticizing a *narrowness* of community. On both counts, however, they were in line with the main interpretations of American character in the 1970s and early '80s, which viewed social atomism rather than conformity as the main problem. Although Lasch and others suggested at times that self-vaunting egoism could go with consumer conformity, the main target of these writers had shifted well away from the seductive, if brittle, 'togetherness' portrayed so vividly by William Whyte in 1956. Whereas Whyte believed Americans suppressed deep needs for individuality, later analysts, such as Slater, Yankelovich, and Bellah, stressed the conflict between modern American culture and deep yearnings for community. Though both groups were concerned with the individual's development, Whyte—like Riesman in 1950—located that development in privacy, in holding something back from society, while the later writers sought it in social involvement.

3

Matters Arising

What are we to make of this body of writing, this stream of generalization? It is, I find, a mixture of distortion and insight. When Philip Slater declared American faces to be monotonously "hard, surly, and bitter," he was surely seeing only what he wanted to see. Yet his picture of Americans isolated and armored in their gadgeted homes stays on my mind so vividly that I believe it—in the case, that is, of *some* Americans.

Likewise Christopher Lasch. Did he really mean that American character trends were as unmitigatedly sick and nasty as he said? And did he actually know that teachers and professional counselors undermined rather than assisted American parents? Yet who of us has not heard the managing but 'liberal' parent who wraps an aggressive coolness in saccharine tones? And is not modern society increasingly one of synthetic and recorded impressions, in which the 'presentation of self' seems to flourish—where the public relations adviser gets an office right next to the boss?

Even David Riesman and his fellow authors of *The Lonely Crowd,* whose description of other-directed character was unusually sensitive and qualified, were hard put to produce convincing examples of it in their follow-up collection of case studies: only two or three fitted the bill.[1] Yet all of us, I imagine, know the kind of modern person—often a teenager and not just American—whose involvement with friends and schoolmates is all bound up with fashion changes and media celebrities; who shares feelings and consumption as ropes to hang on to in an unstructured life.

One reason for the overstatement in these writings was their assumption that American character had one predominant mold or trend (be it Riesman's "other-direction" or Reich's "Consciousness III"). Older types might still be around ("inner-direction" or "Consciousness I and II"); but none of our authors wrote about *several, sharply distinct* character tendencies in modern America, just as few of them discussed differences of class, sex, etc. To some extent, David Riesman, Jules Henry, and Daniel Yankelovich did observe class differences in social character, and David Potter discussed sex differences; but most of the writers assumed that a middle class set a monolithic trend.

The only real attempt in this period to identify a variety of new American character types was one section of a chapter in Max Lerner's *America as a Civilization* (1957). Lerner's types were mainly middle-class responses to bureaucracy, to a culture of marketing, and to a fragmented, mass society. Lerner built on the ideas of Riesman, Whyte, and others, but his analysis was brief.[2]

In one sense, the modern studies of American character look cruder than they are. As I have already suggested, social character is a matter of 'more or less.' Modern American character consists of those attitudes and traits that Americans *tend* to have *more* than other peoples have, or than they themselves used to have. A particular kind of individualism is not something you have or don't have—people practice or believe in it to different extents (as well as showing it in different forms and situations). I think we can assume that all writers reviewed here understood this, but they were apt to use a shorthand style that eclipsed it—to write of this or that attitude or value as if all Americans had it to the same degree. This distortion was usually avoided when writers referred to a statistical survey or case studies of actual people, but many of their assertions were unaccompanied by numbers or specific examples. The wish to command attention by encompassing the people's character in strong, bold strokes was a recipe for overstatement.

It is not surprising, then, that only four of the writers really discussed the prevalence of character type or tendency they had identified.* David Riesman, on "other-direction" in 1950, and Charles

---

*The idea of a social-character *type,* a cluster of traits or attitudes that tend to go together and have a certain prevalence in the population, may seem to contradict the notion that each trait is 'more or less.' The fit between the two ideas is rough and commonsensical rather than precise, and can be expressed in this question: How common are those people who noticeably exhibit a particular set of traits or attitudes?

Reich, on "Consciousness III" in 1970, allowed that their respective types were as yet a minority, concentrated among the more well-to-do young. Christopher Lasch, on the prevalence of narcissism in 1979, was more confusing. Having built up a gloomy picture of narcissism reaching everywhere, at least in the middle classes, he suddenly conceded that "narcissistic disorders" and "narcissistic personalities" might be no more common than before. He believed, however, that narcissists, being well suited to bureaucratic intrigue and "the management of personal impressions," had now got themselves into prominent positions throughout society, reinforcing "narcissistic traits in everyone." Lasch did not explain the difference between people who merely had narcissistic traits and those with narcissistic personalities, nor did he say why the former should increase but not the latter.[3]

The most systematic effort to show the prevalence of a type was Daniel Yankelovich's book of 1981—as one might expect from a pollster. In his survey research, Yankelovich found that 17 percent of employed Americans said they followed a "strong form" of the self-fulfillment ethos—they claimed, that is, to make self-fulfillment a binding principle of their lives. They tended to be younger and more educated than the rest, but a large minority were blue-collar, and they did not all have the same ideas about what self-fulfillment entailed.[4]

What Yankelovich could not support statistically, as his data did not reach back far enough, was his claim that Americans had become *more* preoccupied with self-fulfillment and generally more self-centered than in the early postwar period. Is this in fact true? Does the shift in the social-character literature from concern with conformity to concern with selfishness reflect a real change in American character or merely a change in the writers' sensibilities? I must repeat that writers of the seventies and eighties who sounded the new alarm about egocentrism did not agree on its vintage. This should remind us that a change in what writers say does not automatically and precisely mark a change in what is happening.[5]

My own view of the matter can be summarized in three statements. One, American character has indeed changed since the 1940s, away from extensive involvement in community, but the trend, and its evils, have been exaggerated just as conformism was exaggerated in the 1950s. The very fact that authors found an audience and made a stir decrying egocentrism in the seventies–eighties and conformity in the fifties suggests that in both periods countervailing values were strong. Two, American character has retained in new forms some old tendencies that distinguish it from the social character of other Western peoples. Three, in spite of their differences, all the writers on American character reviewed in these pages shared a common obsession with individualism. This sharpened their hopes and fears, but it also restricted them. Let me elaborate on each of these points.

A survey in the late sixties suggested that 'bureaucratization' did not lead to conformist values as automatically as William Whyte had claimed. Indeed, the study found that employees of larger and more hierarchical organizations were more apt to value "self-direction" and change and to be "intellectually flexible." This was largely due, it seemed, to the sense of freedom created by secure jobs.[6] By the 1960s, too, the decline of anti-intellectualism, while not ensuring the end of fashion-following or 'group think,' was eroding the cruder pressures to conform, such as the old belief that men should leave fancy thoughts and feelings to women.

As marketing pushed into new areas of life, so intellectual and artistic appreciation and psychological experience became objects of consumption. This could still produce conformity to a 'lifestyle' group, but there were more such groups to choose from and, for adults at least, more spaces between them in which to find one's own individuality. It is true that the public face of American life is still very standardized: between McDonald's and Penney's, a paste of lower-middle-class goodies and knickknacks pervades the land. Beneath these uniformities, however, some research has found that parents are readier to let their children follow the inner muse and achieve in more diverse fields than they were in the 1950s.[7]

Do these trends to individuality, most evident in metropolitan America, mean more selfishness and less social bonding? If we look at the 'yuppie' (a term invented by pollsters in the early 1980s), then the answer is yes. To be an archetypal yuppie is more than just being a young urban professional. The picture we usually have is of a single person or one of a couple—without children and not necessarily married—whose total living style is a conscious statement of self. Yuppies may crave genuine achievement at work, but they also want to make money to afford a leisure life that is fun and chic, expressive but also studied.

Yuppies differ from Whyte's young organization man and wife of the 1950s in that they are somewhat less apt to live in the suburbs and do not center their extracurricular activities on Little League, coffee klatches, PTA, and local church or civic affairs.[8] In the middle classes generally, couples have fewer children than they did in the 1950s; more wives go out to work and more adults are single, so they are less apt to be pulled into social activities based on children and neighborhood.

Suburbia itself may have become less communal. This is the line taken by its leading historian, Kenneth Jackson. Like Philip Slater, Jackson sees a mass of "over-equipped" houses and yards which have become "small, private islands." Front-porch society, where everyone met everyone, has been closed down by domestic technology: the automobile, electronic entertainment, and air-conditioning (widespread in houses by the 1960s). Families either vanish indoors (or into their backyards) or whisk themselves away on wheels. Jackson, however, did not consider that technology might produce its own forms of gregariousness, from the many social uses of the telephone to gatherings of youngsters to watch a video or listen to a tape. Jackson did note that shopping malls had become "the new hangouts of the adolescent generation." He also conceded that their suburban elders still went in for "an incredible variety of charitable and voluntary activities."[9]

What evidence, then, is there that American character by and large has become more asocial? The best data on this is the research published in 1981 by Joseph Veroff and associates. In 1976, Veroff et al. surveyed a national cross-section of adult Americans, asking the same questions about their attitudes and lives that had been put to a similar sample in 1957. Compared with their predecessors, it seems that the Americans of 1976 did slightly less visiting to friends' and relatives' homes, and were much less likely to belong to two or more associations (for instance, a school committee, a lodge, a citizens' group, or a church congregation). On the other hand, they were more likely to say that they turned to others for help if they were worried or unhappy—especially to people outside their families. Perhaps this was because fewer of them were married. Virtually all these trends held up at each level of education, though more educated people reported more social activity.

Veroff et al. also found that in the nineteen years between the two surveys, Americans had become more likely to say they valued emotional health and fulfillment and wanted their relations with others to be sensitive and intimate. They now thought more *psychologically,* as opposed to *morally* or *materially*: they were more liable to ask 'How does this feel?' rather than 'Should I?' or 'What do I get?' Although work and family life were both highly valued, people identified themselves and others less by their set roles—being a businessman, a teacher, a wife—and more according to distinctive personal traits. (Reich's Consciousness III was not entirely dead.)

In the authors' view, it was not so much that Americans had become less social; rather, they now depended less on institutions and official roles as a source of relationships and knowledge of others. Instead they relied more on themselves to create the ad hoc networks they wanted. These arrangements, however, were more precarious and more liable to collapse into loneliness.[10]

We don't really know how much the picture has changed since the 1976 survey date. Yankelovich's surveys suggest that Americans may have turned back to more community (see pages 36–37). Nevertheless, Veroff's findings and main interpretations make sense as a statement of general trends. The fall in voting turnout since the nineteenth century, especially marked since 1960, and the decline in church attendance during the 1970s may well reflect a more general decline in civic involvement. At the same time, the new value on psychological health may indeed have produced more searching for 'meaningful' relations with others. The search can be selfish ('I'll relate to you on my terms and when I want to') but not necessarily.

Since the 1950s, several writers on the national character—Jules Henry, Philip Slater, Robert Bellah—have implied they would prefer an America where people were rooted in communities they did not choose, where people inherited a commitment to traditional ties. What they do not say is that such communities can be oppressive, snoopy, and stultifying. Conversely they underestimate the satisfactions of being able to create and select one's social networks, and the sheer vitality of association that comes from working at it out of a fear of being isolated.[11]

I know, for example, a divorcée in Los Angeles whose children are grown and gone and who works all day as a paralegal administrator. She lacks, it is true, a local neighborhood community of the kind that sees when a person needs something and pitches in to help. She has quite strong family ties in various directions, but they are not around the corner. On the other hand, when her youngest child went off to college, she joined a chamber music group and—more distinctively American—she extended a new interest in writing poetry into joining a writers' group, which recently spent a weekend together in the mountains.

On the face of it these were mere hobby groups, which could not impinge on her life at the many points that a village community could. But who knows what the real trade is? If the village is not congenial, one may block it with a shell of emotional privacy, whereas the hobby group may produce kindred spirits whom one opens up to. So much depends on the particular situation and what one wants from a community.

When we move from asking 'How much have Americans changed?' to 'How are they different from non-Americans?' we find more continuity with the past. In my own experience, the writers on social character who best capture a distinctive American style and outlook are commentators who did not stress change and whose studies have been eclipsed in recent decades. I refer particularly to Ralph Barton Perry and Harold Laski in the 1940s and George Pierson in the 1950s and '60s. The phrase that best summarizes what all three saw is *informal dynamism*.

The dynamic part is obvious enough. 'The place is so alive'; 'it makes you feel you can do so much more'—expressions like these are common among British people I know who have visited the United States, whatever their ideologies. Is this just in contrast to a slower Britain? I think not. In 1985 at Smith College, I taught a class of twelve foreign students, mostly graduates in their early twenties, about half from Europe and half from the Third World. What struck them most about their new environment was its competitive individualism, and the sheer pace of life—the amount going on, the work loads, the organized events hatched by this group or that.

From well back in the nineteenth century, America's culture has crackled more than most with the language of energy, speed, and impact: people have prided themselves on being 'go-ahead,' showing 'vim' and 'pep,' and 'hitting the ground running.' Even failure and slowness have been made to sound active: 'We bombed'; 'I'm pacing myself'; and (my favorite Americanism) 'We're getting nowhere fast.'

The commonest historical explanation of American dynamism is probably right. The protracted advance of the frontier, followed by a leaping industrial economy, created a sense of possibility and called out a restless striving. We don't yet know if something happened in the 1970s and '80s to cut off the sources of this dynamism—whether, that is, the sharp decline in U.S. economic self-sufficiency and the shellacking received by average incomes in the past two decades have fundamentally undercut American optimism and expansiveness. (More on this in Chapter 6.) In the meantime, there seems to be plenty of enterprise still about—from doctors and lawyers who dive into real estate on the side to the last policeman I talked with, moonlighting as a chauffeur during the week and a decorator on weekends. In the working class, much of this moneymaking is an attempt to offset the real decline in wage rates; it is also an alternative to moving up a job ladder. Yet American workers retain the notion that individuals control their fate, for they often believe that they *could* have risen higher had they *chosen* to get more education.[12]

American dynamism is not just associated with work. Guided by mass marketing, it has also been channeled into consumption. More recently, in the middle classes, it has found outlets in psychological frontiersmanship: doing more, experiencing more, and feeling good. Whether at work or at play, the idea of 'testing my limits'—a phrase made much of in the seventies—combines old values on achievement with newer notions of self-expansion.

American dynamism, however, gets its distinctive flavor from informality. The trait is shown in boyish enthusiasms; in the hearty 'pleased to meet you' greeting; in the immediate move to first names, a 'let's waste no time' friendliness; in the rapid turnover of slang and the profusion of nicknames, which reach right to the top. Few European statesmen sport the informalized first names of a Jimmy Carter, a Gerry Ford, a Cy Vance, a Cap Weinberger.

American informality signifies a democratic sociability, an impatience with formal status. On riverboats and in hotels, foreign travelers noticed the trait well before the Civil War, but in the twentieth century, mass marketing helped spread it through the society by stressing leisure, fun, and the good effects of smiling. If consumer goods divide people by serving as status symbols, they also connect them. A senior civil servant in Britain's Ministry of Health told me of visiting a big research laboratory in Cincinnati. "Want one of these?" asked the shirtsleeved director as they passed a Coke machine, and so they progressed through the establishment, the Cokes in their hands signaling relaxation and good cheer as they talked with the staff. The Briton could not imagine such a thing happening back home.[13]

In saying all this I do not mean that America has more real equality than most other Western countries (economically it has less). The manager who talks like a 'regular guy' to his employees does not thereby yield power, though he may hear them better if he wants to. The coach who uses earthy language to curse out the squad is no less the squad's boss. And clearly the practice of informality is no cure for profound problems such as racialism. In some ways it may make matters worse by persuading Americans that they are more egalitarian than they really are.

I do not mean, moreover, that America has no pomp and circumstance. Money will out, and gowns will glitter. Gala occasions provide the touch of royalty that Americans often miss. Patriotism, too, requires its great civil rites, supremely exemplified in the President's inauguration. Still, the most uniquely American political celebration, the national party convention, is a wonderful mixture of the formal with the informal, a circus of pompous intoning, frantic bargaining, and organized clowning.

Informal dynamism positions Americans to embrace both individualism and affiliation. It still gets support from the 'I'm as good as you are' assertiveness observed by foreign visitors in the early nineteenth century, but it also shows up in the propensity of Americans to "zap [each other] with friendliness" as a way of heading off possible aggression.[14] In a society of constant movement and many different groups, people cannot take each other for granted. George Pierson may be right in claiming that American sociability has tended to be superficial, but this may simply be because there is so much of it that it cannot all be deep. Around 1960, two comparative studies suggested that Americans were particularly attracted to group activities, from team sports as children to civic associations as adults.[15] If Veroff et al. are right, such involvement has declined more recently, but it may still be higher than that of other Western peoples.

My own observation is that Americans still have some of the special thirst for getting together which Tocqueville noted in the 1830s. The results range from ethnic churches in Pennsylvania mining towns to retirement cooperatives in Florida. As we shall see in the next chapter, Americans have entwined individualism and community in all sorts of ways, and that tradition is far from dead.[16]

What of the social-character studies themselves? What do they tell us as a collective expression of American attitudes? (It is true that two of the works discussed in the last chapter were by Britons—Geoffrey Gorer and Harold Laski—but both were heavily influenced by American writers.) Their most notable feature is their preoccupation with individualism, either its fragility and contradictions or its excesses. In recent times, these concerns have united in the notion that egocentrism and isolation diminish the individual. Many of the writers, indeed, and not just those of the seventies and eighties, share the belief that community in America is shallow in the sense of not giving the individual a deeply rooted identity. This goes with the repeated observation that Americans rather desperately seek the approval of their fellows and lack confidence in how to raise their children.

The fascination with individualism in relation to group life restricts the range of these works. They concentrate on a few major values, and on relationships to others and to self, rather than on the traits and nuances of temperament that a good social novelist picks up. Even *The Lonely Crowd* and *The Culture of Narcissism,* the most complex of the interpretations, restricted themselves in this way. William Whyte, too, lively and sensitive writer though he was, trained his antennae on the delicate relations between corporate, suburban Americans and the organization about them rather than spotting and linking up a medley of character traits.[17]

These studies are also connected by the four fears that I mentioned at the outset: the fear of being owned and controlled; the fear of falling apart; the fear of winding down, of losing vigor and momentum; and the fear of falling away from a past virtue and promise.

The fear of being owned was most obvious in the 1940s and '50s concern with conformity: a kind of ownership by the group. It appeared in the worry of Riesman et al. (1950) that Americans had lost psychological space. White-collar work had taken over and drained their emotional life by requiring them to be personable "gladhanders." On a philosophical note, William Whyte (1956) expressed a fear of being owned when he declared that the "organization man" had lost the sense of controlling his own destiny.[18]

David Potter's pioneering essay on "American Women and the American Character" (1962) applied the issue of being owned to gender when it observed that a male-dominated consumer system controlled women's identity.[19] This line of thinking was widened by Charles Reich's *The Greening of America* (1970) to include almost everyone, the corporate subjects of imposed roles and "false consciousness."

The fear of being owned also runs through Christopher Lasch's concept (1979) of a capitalist "bureaucracy" that invades the family and creates a diminished and dependent psyche. In Lasch's book, old American suspicions of the state teamed up with a new-style, psychological assault on consumer capitalism. Corporate planners, along with their allies in the social sciences, were accused of manipulating attitudes and emotions. Although Lasch scorned the 'new left' of the 1960s, his attack owed much to its view that modern technocrats advanced their controlling doctrines in the guise of 'value-free' social science. Whatever they liked they called 'functional'; whatever they disliked was called 'dysfunctional' or sick. This critique, ironically, was very similar to the charge against personnel managers and their social-science mentors made years before by that Time Inc. business writer William Whyte.[20]

The fear of falling apart, applied to America as a whole, appeared most obviously in the belaboring of egocentrism in the seventies and eighties. But it appeared earlier too, in David Potter's worry about the lack of class ties, in George Pierson's recognition of the antisocial side of American mobility, in Jules Henry's allusion to teenage distrust. On a personality level, Daniel Yankelovich (1981) evoked the specter of falling apart when he described an imperialism of "needs," commanding the individual to live it up in all directions.

David Riesman's similar portrait (1980) of the "over-optioned life," spreading emotion too thin in the hunt for new experiences, took him back thirty years to his early study, *The Lonely Crowd.* Although the "other-directed" characters of that book were pleasure seekers too, they were also believed to be emotionally passive and shallow; conformists who were nonetheless unable to get really close to one another, they felt an underlying fear of isolation. Riesman's Americans of 1981 seemed less bound by group norms, but his own analysis had not changed all that much. He continued to believe that social pressures to have fun in prescribed ways, be they from a peer group or the mass culture, threatened individual spontaneity as well as the self-discipline of the craftsman. For Riesman, as for Yankelovich and Lasch, modern hedonism involved a 'falling apart' and a 'being owned': its very license caused diffuse anxiety and a sense of aimlessness, yet it was also a weighty cultural imposition.[21]

Winding down and falling away recur, too, in these studies. Margaret Mead, the first writer in our series, expressed both fears as much as anyone. Toward the end of her wartime analysis of American character, Mead suddenly took fright. "For the first time in American history, we have had a generation raised by parents who did not see themselves as knights of a shining cause." The rot had started in World War I. "The cheap, shoddy slogans of the commercial world, hastily pressed into service to rally a surprised nation to arms" had sold the war to Americans as just one more quick victory, a score along the way. The war involved no great sacrifice, and after it, Americans betrayed their idealism in rejecting the League of Nations.

What would this "failure of will and purpose" produce? A generation "unfit to lead in building a new world"? The saving factor, for Mead, was the Protestant pattern of child-rearing, a tradition which was strongest in America. In spite of their political failures, American parents had continued, in a hundred little ways, to instill a sense of personal responsibility, to encourage their children to go beyond their own achievements and believe in social progress, recognizing there was "no excuse for standing still or going backward." None of this, though, entirely reassured Mead. She still felt she had to call on Americans to reach beneath their "passive gadget-born attitudes" to their essential, puritan "mixture of practicality and faith in God" (Oliver Cromwell's "trust in God . . . and keep your powder dry"). This would only work if big organizations, be they government or business, let people use their own initiative and ingenuity.[22]

But was the puritanism still there? Riesman and Whyte in the fifties, Lasch and Yankelovich in the late seventies and early eighties, all claimed that Americans had lost (or were losing) a 'Protestant Ethic' of work, self-denial, and thrift—they did not point out that this had been a matter of comment and speculation since at least the early nineteenth century.[23] In different ways, also, a number of writers suggested that Americans had lost authenticity and directness, had become more artificial and packaged; they were conditioned by agents—advertising, therapy, child-rearing manuals—that vaguely seemed less genuine than parental instinct.

The result was a nation of manipulated manipulators who had lost a stable sense of reality. Psychologically they had become less secure and therefore weaker, for their identity depended either on a shifting group or on themselves alone. The theme of falling away from a past state of virtue was particularly pronounced when writers looked back to the Republic's early decades and found there a better balance between individualism and community.[24]

The four fears come together most keenly in Lasch's *Culture of Narcissism*. His modern characters are deeply antisocial yet *psychologically owned*—their drives shaped and manipulated—by the economic power system of advanced capitalism. They have lost moral integrity, a sense of inner cohesion: their very anxieties are vague and diffuse. As individual competitors they are vigorous indeed, but it is a kind of vigor that diminishes the nation's productivity as competitive show replaces solid achievement. A jeremiad on the "spiritual desolation of modern life," Lasch's book was attacked by critics for grotesquely pathologizing Americans, but that did not stop its becoming a leading nonfiction seller (seven weeks among the top fifteen in the *New York Times* survey of U.S. bookstores).

The four fears had also converged in Vance Packard's book of 1960, *The Waste Makers*. Vance Packard deserves notice as America's best-known popular sociologist over the past thirty years. From *The Hidden Persuaders* (1957) and *The Status Seekers* (1959) to *Our Endangered Children* (1983), his books mainly deal with threats—especially threats in the form of soft-voiced manipulators.[25] Packard's statement in *The Waste Makers* supplied a link between Riesman's consumers and Yankelovich's high-spending self-fulfillers. It also developed a theme of American critics in the late 1950s who lamented materialist 'privatism' among the nation's young suburbanites. Mixing vivid social horror stories with clearly distilled statistics, Packard claimed that a new consumer self-indulgence had made Americans impervious to the claims of community and people in distress. The pressure on parents—both parents—to go out and earn more to buy more damaged family life and contributed to juvenile delinquency.

These observations invoked the fear of falling apart, but they also involved the fear of being psychologically owned, for Packard attributed consumer hedonism largely (though not entirely) to the designs of corporate management. Packard expressed, too, a fear of falling away, for he believed that American character had changed abruptly in the consumer boom following World War II. As technology enabled producers to make more goods with fewer workers, so business tried to keep up profits and employment by getting people to buy more. This required a new ethic of "prodigality" and "pleasure-mindedness." Like Riesman, Packard did not say why the new consumer character arrived in the 1940s and '50s rather than, say, the 1920s. He was probably a better prophet than historian: he was one of the first popular writers of his time to assert that spiraling consumption would endanger natural resources. In this, as in the "new softness" that he found about him, Packard expressed a fear of winding down.[26]

It would be easy to suppose that writers who take a more kindly view of American character have no connection with the four fears. This is not true, as we saw in the case of Margaret Mead. Even the upbeat Ralph Barton Perry, writing just after Mead in the late forties, was responding to American society's pressure on the individual (the threat of being owned) and its competitiveness and "centrifugal expansion" (the appearance of falling apart). His concept of "collective individualism" was a way of coming to terms with both.

Again, David Potter's articles of the early sixties were quite tolerant of modern American individuality, but he was worried nonetheless about modern, liberal types of conformists. Too often, in his view, they conformed to a libertarianism that abetted selfishness and license. Potter simultaneously gave voice to the fear of being owned (by group pressures) and the fear of falling apart. In the early sixties too, Seymour Martin Lipset's optimistic essay stressing a productive continuity in American character was a deliberate reply to the fear of decline and the specter of a new kind of conformity raised by Riesman and Whyte.[27]

I have said that modern studies of American character do not have to be negative to engage with the four fears; but most of them are just that. Of the twenty interpretations reviewed in the last chapter and this, I judge eleven to be predominantly unfavorable: conveying, that is, contemporary national character to American readers in a bad light, whether intentionally or not. Six are mainly neutral or mixed. Only three—Laski and Perry in 1949, Lipset in 1963—are essentially favorable.[28]

These less than rosy results tie in with the findings of a five-nation comparison done in 1959–60. When asked, "What are the things about this country that you are most proud of?" Americans were much more apt than the others to cite their political traditions and institutions. They were the least likely to mention their qualities as a people.[29] The findings do *not* show that Americans were less proud of their qualities than the others; they do indicate that Americans were unusually prone to praise their political institutions above their character.

This helps to explain the fear of falling away that recurs in the American social-character studies. The veneration given by Americans to their long-standing, dramatically created Constitution causes anxiety about upholding the ideals and virtues it represents. Amid the perplexities of the modern world, it is easy for Americans to believe that they are failing to fulfill their eighteenth-century heritage. Of the eight writers in my survey who *explicitly* disapproved of the main trends in American character, just three—Jules Henry in 1962, Philip Slater and Michael Lewis in the 1970s—stressed continuity rather than decline, and even they believed that matters had become somewhat worse.

Another way of looking at all this is to suggest that Americans have often targeted criticism onto their personal and spiritual qualities as a way of avoiding real challenge to their basic institutions. The implied solution is self-redemption, plus maybe some revamping of school and college programs, rather than painful and divisive efforts to rearrange political structures and economic rewards. In our stable of writers on modern American character, a number attributed its tensions and defects to the economic system, but only Vance Packard and Philip Slater (in his revised, 1976 edition) made substantial suggestions for reforming that system. Of course, there are many other kinds of writers who do criticize specific features of the economic and political system, but their following might be greater if Americans did not have so strong a tradition of blaming their profoundest problems on individual moral character rather than on institutions.[30]

Numerous surveys have shown that Americans are the most religious Western people, in belief and in numbers going to church. This is quite aside from the enormous, California-led development of psycho-spiritual 'awareness' groups, meditation schools, etc. The American social-character industry complements this religiosity, for it, too, is concerned with souls and values and 'consciousness.' It is a secular and eclectic church.

4

Community

[We feminists want] a dialectical tension between freedom that does not entail isolation and community that does not enforce uniformity.

Kathy E. Ferguson, *The Feminist Case Against Bureaucracy* (1984)

We were a circle of trust, a sort of band of brothers. Those people, the people that I struggled with, and went to jail with, and went to lunch counters and on the freedom rides with, these folks really became my family. I think Martin Luther King, Jr., himself, sort of being the symbolic leader, gave all of us . . . a sort of sense of somebodyness. Being involved tended to free you . . . you saw yourself as the free man, as the free agent, able to act.

After what Martin Luther King, Jr., had to say, what he did, as an individual you couldn't feel alone again.

John Lewis, on the 1950s–60s civil rights movement (1984)[1]

Both these statements, from sources so at odds with so much in America, are quintessentially American. Both of them reflect the special experiences of a distinctive 'undergroup'; but they also express the dual yearning for individualism and community that keeps coming back in these pages. The curious thing is that writing on American character does not say a great deal about this dualism—at least not intentionally. None of the social-character studies discussed here explores the many intricate connections between different types of

American individualism and the drive to associate, to join and have ties, with people outside one's own immediate family. No history book, either, has explicitly examined these connections over a range of periods.

I want, therefore, to look at six historical situations, and a seventh, contemporary one, that have braided individualism with the call to affiliate. Although they extend from the seventeenth century to the twentieth, all of them have left their mark on modern America.[2]

PURITANISM IN SEVENTEENTH-CENTURY MASSACHUSETTS

The Congregationalist community founded by John Winthrop and his companions was a testament to individual conscience, seeking escape from the spiritual corruption and interference of the Anglican Church and the English court. The Massachusetts Bay Colony also reflected a more secular individualism: it offered new opportunities to prosper, command status, and wield influence. Yet the Puritans of seventeenth-century Massachusetts had a strong sense of local community. They huddled together in their church democracy, not only as a defense against the frightful pagan wilderness but as a carryover from their English resistance to royal power.

Theologically, the Puritan settlers threaded collectivism through the very eye of their individualism. They believed that the faith which led to salvation was awarded by God's grace; it was a veiled and personal force. Individual prosperity and good works done for others were some indicator of future salvation but were neither proof nor guarantee of it. To believe that good works could *obtain* grace was to commit the sin of Arminianism—a sin of pride, the blasphemous exaltation of human will—which Winthrop had found among the high priests of Anglicanism in London.

Yet inward-looking devotion joined with a kind of totalitarianism, for securing morality in one's neighbors, was a sign of faith within oneself. The community was collectively responsible for obeying God, who was liable to reward obedience with general prosperity and punish disobedience with afflictions—bad crops, perhaps, or an epidemic. The result was a dual concentration on personal states of mind and communal conduct (which in turn led to a collective responsibility for the sick and the destitute). The theology encouraged economic achievement yet sought to limit its ultimate importance.

The Anne Hutchinson crisis of the 1630s exposed the tension between Puritan individualism and Puritan communalism. In claiming that only personal revelation could show who was likely to be saved, Hutchinson denied that the church community and its leaders could know the probable recipients of God's grace. Good works, she said, were no sign of it. When the General Court condemned her for heresy, it did so in anger at the unseemly assertiveness of a woman who had used her position as a midwife to organize a subversive discussion group.

Even here, then, an individualist's revolt took place in a framework of meetings and relationships. At the same time, by challenging the church's authority to monitor how people lived, she left a place for economic individualism too. When Hutchinson was banished and made the trek to Rhode Island, a disproportionate number of her supporters and companions were well-to-do members of the Boston elite, especially merchants involved in foreign trade. Though they tended to be church members and public officeholders, they had probably had enough of church controls, especially the rules against 'usury.'

At Salem in 1692, the teenage girls who sent twenty 'witches' to their deaths played out a twisted parody of Hutchinson's revolt. On the face of it, the young witch-accusers were collectivists, supercharged by a group hysteria. They lived in the most traditional part of Salem, and their victims tended to be eccentrics or people with mercenary reputations. Yet in claiming, each one, to be attacked by witchcraft, and in being allowed to rest their cases on lies or fantasies rather than objective evidence, they purported to have personal hot lines from the supernatural—to see, by Satanic revelation, what the court could not see but accepted. Armed with this power, they used it, consciously or not, to manipulate the authorities that had long repressed them. Displaying themselves with cries and moans, each of them found a stage, sometimes individually at home, sometimes together in court.

For reasons of its own, Salem was a particularly strife-ridden and neurotic community. Elsewhere in Massachusetts, adolescent revolt was more direct and frivolous. Thrown together by cramped and communal housing, young men and women sometimes evaded the stern regime of their parents in evening excursions to the tavern, in frolics and carousing, and (among girls) in secret reading of bawdy gynecological tracts. Although most of this was group behavior, it made a space for individual ringleaders and pranksters who led on their little bands, just as Anne Hutchinson, in her weightier realm, had made a personal instrument of a midwife's discussion group.[3]

THE OUTLOOK OF BENJAMIN FRANKLIN

As colonial New England moved toward the Revolution, a covert Arminianism—the belief that deeds could secure salvation—gained ground. Movements such as Hutchinson's were passing reactions against this, and her revolt, as we have seen, supported economic individualism.

Down in Philadelphia, the deism of Benjamin Franklin reflected the trends. Writing the first page of his *Autobiography* in 1771, Franklin thanked "Providence" for his "constant good fortune," but he was still proud to have risen from "poverty and obscurity" to "affluence and some degree of celebrity in the world." As a young man in 1728, he wrote his own epitaph, likening himself to a book that would "appear once more, in a new and more perfect Edition, corrected and amended by the Author" (i.e., God); but around the same time he also devised his typically systematic agenda for attaining "moral perfection" on earth. The scheme included the humble imitation of Jesus and Socrates, but it left no place for prayer and receiving grace. Perfection, it implied, would depend on conduct, on Benjamin Franklin. In 1736, he wrote, "God gives all things to industry."

Four words supply the key to Franklin's character: wealth, reputation, curiosity, and improvement. As a versatile and successful printer, Franklin enjoyed finding business and turning a profit, but he also valued wealth as a means, a source of independence for doing what he wanted to do, and a shield against temptation. It was easier, he said, for a rich man to be honest than a poor one.

He prized reputation, too, as a satisfaction in itself but also as a form of capital which could secure custom and influence. One of his most modern characteristics was his fascination with the art of presenting oneself. The virtues on show were not exactly today's—thrift and industry were more important—but the purpose was much the same: to impress customers and creditors, and get people to do what you wanted. Franklin did this in part by showing he could do what *others* wanted, that he was able and ready to *provide,* be it wagons for an army or an association to prevent and fight fires.

Much of what Franklin said and did seems to have been 'done for a purpose,' seldom a selfish one but usually with self-interest in train. In his *Autobiography,* he tells of forming the Junto, a discussion club of self-educated artisans and others, for "mutual improvement" and in a "sincere spirit of enquiry." The club's standing rules, however, suggest that the main purpose of the club was the material advancement of its members by trading information. A brilliant Enlightenment rationalist who was also a mobile operator in a new, metropolitan world, Franklin was forever inventing structures and systems to help him move forward. Even talk and conversation were, for Franklin, an art, to be analyzed and used with cunning tact. Franklin was a proto–Dale Carnegie, a prophet of "how to win friends and influence people." Full of tips on how to get people to cooperate and work contentedly, he was a pioneer of what today would be called 'human relations' and 'positive reinforcement.'

One might conclude from all this that Franklin was at heart a pure individualist who merely used social skills and contacts for his own ends. In a brilliant passage written more than half a century ago, the historian Carl Becker noted Franklin's inner distance from the people and events he so energetically met; the affairs of the world were games to be played well, but deep down, Franklin was detached from them, an amused observer. Only science and the natural world engaged all his passion, without subterfuge or guile.[4] In matters great and small, a powerful curiosity pervaded Franklin's life: put aside the usual list of his experiments and inventions and simply picture him in London, listening to the great evangelical preacher George Whitefield and retreating backward to calculate how many people could hear him at one time (over thirty thousand was his estimate).

At the very least, then, Franklin's individualism was not one of mere self-obsession; the image of the inquisitive, active spectator is of a man looking *out* upon the world. But of course there is much more to it than this. If Franklin cultivated contacts for his own ends, he was able to do so because it came easily to him; the simple 'republican' manners that so impressed the French were part of a genial and sociable character, trusting enough to be taken advantage of more than once.

His pursuit of self-improvement, too, reflected a wider value on improvement per se. His repeated statement that "doing good to man" was "the most acceptable service to God" should not be discounted. Franklin's inventiveness constantly sought social outlets, from the 1754 military "Plan of Union" between the colonies to his designs for lighting and cleaning city streets. His refusal to patent his famous stove seems to have been based on genuine public spirit and a compulsion for spreading knowledge. All this led him into rich and varied associations with others—his fire company's provision for a "social evening" of useful talk was very Franklin. Association was part of his lifeblood, a natural and happy means of solving problems and mastering the world.[5]

NORTHEASTERN REVIVALISM IN THE 1830s

Franklin's spiritual self-reliance did not become the predominant Protestant doctrine until long after his death in 1790. As late as 1825, in Rochester, New York, the Presbyterian church affirmed that only God, not man, could alter the spiritual state of an individual and the condition of society. Since the 1790s, however, evangelicals had been challenging these beliefs. In his celebrated sermon of November 28, 1830, the revivalist minister Charles Finney told a rapt congregation of Rochester Presbyterians that God had made man a "moral free agent." Provided they sought God's help by surrendering to Him, they could make themselves over.

Salvation, new-style, required individual willpower but it still needed collective action, too. Just as Benjamin Franklin had declared that "virtuous men ought to league together," so Finney called Christians to unite against sin. If they did, the millennium could be realized in three months! Finney foreshadowed the modern American longing for quick results and the fascination with changing 'hearts and minds.' He also tapped a sense of infinite possibility, which coursed through American culture in the 1830s. Two of his favorite texts from the Bible were "Behold, I come swiftly" and "With God nothing shall be impossible."

The 1830s were a time of unusual economic expansion, especially for the canal town of Rochester. In this climate, Finney's evangelism made a double offer. One side of it was a spiritualized version of the self-made man. Finney himself was just this. The son of poor farmers, he had studied law until a dramatic conversion experience changed his life. (His sermons, appropriately, built up their emotional force through a step-by-step logic, which fitted legal as well as Puritan traditions.) In telling his audience that they could seize a spiritual initiative, could find God and remake themselves, Finney spoke the language of entrepreneurs who wanted to go out and raise capital to raise themselves.

Yet the other side of his message was an antidote to economic individualism. At a time when cheap manufactured goods were transforming middle-class living standards, Finney and other evangelists attacked the vices of materialism. Against the strain of 'getting on,' the evangelists offered the fierce relief of turning from a dependence on luxuries to a dependence on God, while preserving individual choice and action. Moreover, in terrifying their audiences with the prospect of damnation and the urgency of coming to God, Finney and other revivalists threw them together for support. Public prayer in Finney's services was intensively subjective but also communal; large numbers of confessed sinners, some weeping, came forward to sit on the 'anxious bench' at the front.

Finney gave a strong community role to women, ardent busybodies who would proselytize other women when their husbands were at work, to get them to come to church and bring their husbands too. The numerous societies spawned by evangelism—distributing Bibles, preaching temperance, reforming prisons and asylums—provided communities of dedicated action for women as well as men. Within these battalions of the Lord, a middle-aged housewife or a young city bank clerk could find fellowship and status.

In his study of the Rochester revival, the historian Paul Johnson argued that the movement was an unconscious form of class control. He noted that it struck first and most the households of rising manufacturers, master craftsmen, and related businessmen. It did so at just the time when apprentices and employees, who traditionally lived under their master's roof, were tending to live on their own. Revivalism, with its stress on temperance and industriousness, was relayed to the workers as a way of controlling their culture and curbing their convivial drinking when they no longer lived in the family orbit of their employers. In support of his argument, Johnson showed that those business householders who had no employees living in were particularly apt to 'get religion.'

There may be some truth to Johnson's theory, but his own data shows that Rochester's revival appealed disproportionately more to middle-class households that had no paying 'boarders' or living-in relatives (a sister-in-law or a grandfather) than to households that contained no employees. My inference is that revivalism offered ascetic solace to the new business-class nuclear family—relief from its isolation and the strains of economic independence.[6]

OVERLAND COMPANIES IN THE MID-NINETEENTH CENTURY

Although evangelism made many eddies into American culture, church membership before the Civil War never exceeded 15 percent of the national population. Yet in secular enterprises too, individualism and the claims of community tumbled about each other, sometimes drawing apart and sometimes fusing. This happened in the overland companies, associations of settlers heading west, having formed up for mutual assistance under elected commanders.

In its origins and main purpose, the overland company was merely the administrative structure around a wagon train, an instrument for the self-interest of the families and individuals that made up the train. It was a temporary organization, and people frequently left one company for another at the different staging points along the great trails west. But instrumental organizations have a way of generating communities. There was a trace of this even in some of the formal constitutions signed by company members. On May 9, 1849, the members of one wagon train association agreed unanimously:

> We the subscribers, members of the Green and Jersey Company of emigrants to California, now rendezvoused at St. Joseph; in view of the long and difficult journey before us, are satisfied that our own interests require for the purpose of safety, convenience, *good feeling,* and what is of the utmost importance, the prevention of unnecessary delay, the adoption of strict rules and regulations to govern us during our passage; and we do by our signatures to this resolution, *pledge ourselves each to the other,* that we will abide by all the rules and regulations that may be made by a vote of the majority of the company, for its regulation during our passage; that *we will manfully assist and uphold any authorized officer* in his exertions to strictly enforce all such rules as may be made.
>
> And further, in case any members of the company, by loss of

oxen or mules, by breaking of wagon, robbery by the Indians, or in fact from any cause whatever beyond their control, are deprived of the ability to proceed with the company in the usual manner, *we pledge ourselves never to desert them, but from our means and resources to support and assist them* to get through to Sutter's Fort, and in fact, *we pledge ourselves to stand by each other, under any justifiable circumstance to the death.* [My italics.]

These constitutions often failed. A family with illness or a broken axle might be left behind, or the men might quarrel and divide over the best route to take. Yet within the overland associations smaller communities were constantly forming. Company rules often upheld the right of friends to eat together in camp and keep their wagons together (over half the families trekking west in midcentury traveled in extended kin groups). Along the way, too, networks of affection and emotional support sprang up. These were especially important for the women, struggling to keep their children healthy and safe as the plodding but dangerous ox hoofs moved the caravan forward at two miles an hour. At the trail's end, or when a group left the company, there were often embraces and tears. The intensity of a community does not always depend on its longevity.[7]

PROGRESSIVE LEADERS OF THE 1890s AND 1900s

Leaders of America's burgeoning reform movements at the turn of the century were, by and large, a gregarious lot. From Brand Whitlock's youthful membership in a club of Chicago reporters to the brain trust used by Cleveland mayor Tom Johnson, the habit of getting together nurtured the Progressives with ideas as well as friendship. By correspondence and travel, their communities stretched over distance too. For instance, in the Lake Erie region of Michigan and Ohio, a remarkable group of radical mayors knew each other and shared mentors such as Henry George and the inspiring Illinois governor John P. Altgeld.

No one ideology commanded all Progressives, but the historian Daniel Rodgers has noted their "language of social bonds," attacking the individualist belief that society was not responsible (either causally or morally) for one person's becoming a millionaire and another a beggar. In stressing collective responsibilities, some Progressives looked to the federal government and a rather impersonal national-ism, but many wanted to revive local communities and humanize and beautify the city.

Admittedly, local reform efforts were not always the friend of social bonds. Moves to hire officials by examination and substitute citywide elections for the old ward boss system elevated a bureaucracy based on 'business principles' above a politics knit by ethnic loyalties. On the other hand, the slum settlement houses created genuine relation-ships between working-class women and the ladies who ran the houses; they also provided contacts and friendships among educated women who wanted to get involved in social action. Many reformers found comfort in such friendships; they meant a lot when acquain-tances from a more conventional past were giving them the cold shoulder.

Yet in their very zeal for union, the Progressives explicitly sought to preserve the individual from being swamped by the new indus-trial empires and the political machines. Progressive leaders applied the same wariness to their own lives. In fighting to regulate busi-ness and make public officials more accountable, the Progressives saw themselves as doughty moral Davids against the Goliaths of corrupt power. Social action was a new frontier, and the Progres-sives were intrepid pioneers, leading the people from far enough ahead to be lone figures. These images maintained a romantic indi-vidualism amid the demands of modern, mass organization. Pro-gressives wanted to reshape and *use* organization; they also wanted to keep their identity free of it.

In a recent study of Progressive autobiographies, a British historian, Valerie Watt, has discovered that the writers tended to stress their independence and rebelliousness from an early age. In building up their heroic stature, they sometimes denied and sometimes exalted the importance of their ancestry. Occasionally they did both! The Wisconsin Progressive James Frear declared:

> Never have I leaned on my ancestors, because every American is judged by his own course and action . . . Yet I am moved to say that my genealogy dates back directly to a Revolutionary captain who, while leading his Connecticut company in battle, was killed and I assume was one of the heroes who helped make possible this great government under which we live.

He went on to list other public services given by his ancestors. Frear, and those like him, supplemented their ambiguous relationship with contemporary society by seeking a *historic* community of kin. This gave distinctive meaning to their own lives while placing them in a collective, American experience.[8]

DEPARTMENT STORE SALESWOMEN, 1890s–1930s

From well before the Civil War, militant workers had based their resistance to employer demands and wage cuts on a mixture of solidarity with a craft tradition of independence. In the late nineteenth century too, the farmers of the Populist party built their ideology of the independent yeoman and their system of social clubs and mutual aid into a political attack on 'the interests.' In our own time, the civil rights movement of the 1950s–60s enhanced its members' self-respect and dignity through the very act of joining together to claim freedom and citizenship (see John Lewis's comment at the head of this chapter). The same is true of other political underdog movements, from Chicanos to Native Americans to feminists.[9]

But individualism and mutuality also became entangled when workers simultaneously resisted and supported corporate organization. Between 1890 and 1940, in the great new houses of consumer capitalism, department store saleswomen maintained a three-cornered relationship between the profit goals of management (the organization), obligations to each other (the community), and their own aspirations (individualism). A penetrating study of saleswomen's "work culture," 1890–1940, by Susan Benson suggests that these three values supported yet opposed each other—though this is not how Benson herself puts it.[10]

In some respects, saleswomen and management had compatible attitudes. The job was less menial than being a domestic servant. Although poorly paid, it offered somewhat better chances of promotion than other white-collar jobs for women. It encouraged the saleswoman to acquire middle-class styles, to take the initiative with customers, and project the glamour of consumption. Saleswomen often took pride in developing their own distinctive sales 'personalities,' and they liked to be well informed about their products. To interfere in each other's selling to a particular customer was taboo.

All this made for individualism. But their salesmanship was collective too. In off moments the women would sometimes play customer, acting out a selling routine, which enabled them to share techniques and initiate newcomers while mimicking the clientele and each other. Outside the store they often (not always) showed patriotism toward it, extolling its products to friends.

Within each department a strong community developed. In virtual defiance of their supervisors, the women would huddle and gossip, and sometimes bring in homemade food. If a comrade was sick or destitute, they would help her out. Each department had its idea of 'the stint'—a good day's selling for each person, which should not be exceeded by too much. In a survey of one store in the late thirties, most women said they would not leave their department for a promotion. In contrast with the male management, the department was very much a community of women; male clerks who strayed there were quickly made to feel out of place. If it was a culture of consumer femininity, it also supported a certain feminism, swift to attack sexual harassment and ready (before the Nineteenth Amendment) to talk about getting the vote.

After the thirties, says Benson, new selling methods, centered on display and self-service, eroded the department store community, which had depended on personal selling and a closely grouped sales force. In a sense, though, the erosion was not new. From well back in the nineteenth century, managers and technology had threatened the solidarity of workers. As early as 1900, department store managers tried to discourage saleswomen from aiding each other financially. Long before this, on a wider front, business-class reform groups attacked working-class saloon culture on behalf of family values and individual productivity: they pressed workingmen to stay home and sober when not under discipline in the factory. In the factory itself, speedups and the sheer noise of machinery often interfered with shop-floor cultures. So, more recently, have assembly-line techniques, which now extend from manufacturing to fast-food chains. Many manual jobs, however, still provide space for work-floor communities—in warehousing, for example; in some automated plants; among hospital workers.[11]

FACULTY LIFE IN THE MODERN LIBERAL ARTS COLLEGE

America's elite colleges and universities brew powerful mixtures of 'joining' and independence, trust and distrust. The individualism found at Smith College by my foreign students (p. 45) sometimes led to crude attempts at trading and manipulation ("If you help me with my French paper, you can come home with me on the weekend"); it also led to genuine cooperation (informal study groups sprawled over the dorm floor). But let me focus on faculty life as a visiting scholar has seen it at several institutions.

In addition to regular classes and committee meetings, each semester seems to be full of collective events—from special seminars to departmental dinners to all the cultural activities (concerts, plays, and the like) that an intellectual community anywhere is apt to produce. If the location is a college town (historically common in America because of the many church sects and other founders of small colleges), a faculty member's colleagues will often be his or her neighbors, and maybe fellow parents at the high school. In social history books such 'cross-cutting' relationships are generally supposed to be a good thing, the hallmark of a close and warm community. But for some the diet is a little wearing: 'you always meet the same people,' 'you can't get away from your colleagues.'

These reactions are not seen as heresy, for the drive to achieve is a very personal matter. The American academic principle that permanent tenure is a prize, for which younger faculty insecurely strive, merely reinforces the value attached to research and writing, and both of these are largely private acts. Publication, not teaching, is the crucial determinant of who gets tenure and, after that, of when a person is made a full professor, and who then gets a 'named chair.' The 'incentive' schemes, practiced at some institutions, of awarding pay bonuses according to volume or quality of publication are practically unheard of in Europe. Such awards are made, of course, because good scholarship redounds to the credit of the college and the department, but the scholar concerned will probably be more interested in impressing members of his discipline across the country.

In spite of all this, the American belief in sharpening performance through feedback and analysis plays upon teaching as well. Most European faculties would be embarrassed by American-style efforts to evaluate and reward good teaching through student questionnaires and 'outstanding teacher' awards. Certainly I can't imagine a British university requiring its department heads to visit the classes of junior colleagues, a practice at some American colleges.

As if to compensate for these pressures, the system does its bit to recognize informal and democratic relations between faculty members—almost everyone, after all, is a 'professor' of some kind, unlike academic staff in Europe. And in a good American faculty, professors take genuine interest in one another's work and share their research and ideas about teaching. Yet every so often, when a difficult tenure decision comes before a department's tenured faculty or a higher college committee, the department will be rent by bitterness. (If the candidate for tenure teaches well but has not written much, students, too, may join issue by organizing a vehement petition to keep the candidate on.) Another aggravation, and not just on tenure questions, is the conflict between the will of a powerful department chair or dean and the collegial belief that a properly constituted faculty body should make the decisions.

Here, then, as much as anywhere in the United States, collegiality rubs up against individualism, and informal relations coexist with formal rules and procedures. A society of contentious minorities requires informal give-and-take, but it also demands clear and common standards for doing its business.[12]

I don't wish to press these cases into a tidy, linear theory of change. One can, of course, see long-term changes in American individualism and community. Notions of self-realization have become more secular. Communities have become more specialized—associations for this or that rather than entities embracing home and work together. But these changes characterize the modern world, not just America.

I want, instead, to treat these seven experiences as legacies and lessons. Against those politicians who vaguely invoke community while implying that self-serving individualism is *the* American way and will automatically enrich everyone, my interpretation of the past shows that American individualism has often involved a great deal of organized caring for others. That caring, however, has to be worked at, for individualism can indeed become selfishness, whatever doctrines it adopts.

There are other lessons too. What Robert Bellah called "expressive individualism" goes back to the Puritans' 'inspired heart' yet was always more entangled with Bellah's "utilitarian individualism" than he recognized. Genuine gregariousness is not always separable from the use of others to get on, and business organizations do not necessarily lack a community soul, though the soul they get may not be what management has in mind.

Even the Progressives' delight in their ancestors has contemporary relevance. Against the claims, heard so often today, that Americans lack interest in their history, the modern fascination with genealogy and finding one's place of origin in the Old World shows a wish to root one's identity in the past and in others. So does that unique American institution, the college or high school class reunion. The reunion is at once a personal and collective stocktaking, a personal search for collective roots, and a collective search for the meaning of individual lives.[13]

What, then, are the main historic links between American individualism and the urge to affiliate? One is that of *compensation,* a check against the pull of loneliness, selfishness, and aggression that lies within individualism. A closely related link is that of *structure* and *status.* In a society of fast-moving competitors, people crave the order and belonging that many kinds of association give; they can also make a mark within the group. Another link is *effectiveness.* Americans have done a lot of voluntary teaming up to get things done, especially when government is weak or unpopular, as it so often has been. By bidding people to measure themselves by results, and by telling them that individuals can make a difference (if they get their collective act together), traditional individualism directly feeds group action. But this blurs at the margin into an *expressive* connection too. For many Americans, personal expansiveness—the drive to experience more, know more, embrace and incorporate more of the world—leads to involvement with others, as much through argument and contention as through agreement. Reaching out to others can be just another form of control and acquisition, but it can also be a way of opening and enlightening the self.[14]

In suggesting that all these connections are still part of American culture, I do not mean that community is everywhere triumphant. I must repeat: its engagement with individualism is often ambiguous; and quick changes in a person's situation can sharply alter the community presence. A New York lawyer recently told me of moving from being a law partner to being vice-chairman of a savings bank. He missed, he said, the collegiality of the law firm, of being able to drop in on a fellow partner and talk about a case or the work in general.

Now he was a boss, isolated in a corner office. There were committee meetings, but they were just that—committee meetings.*

At the other extreme, individualism itself can be a mythic sham. How else can one view the highly drilled state-college football band, swaying in a choreographed routine, while it plays "I'll Do It My Way"? Yet for all its regimentation, American football itself makes sophisticated provision for individualism on the field; and with its heavy use of substitutes and ancillaries—from trainers to cheerleaders—the college or high school football team is often the center of a large and vital community. There are, indeed, towns in America where high school football games are the main meeting point between working class and middle class.[15]

A few years ago, I dined in a college-town restaurant with a self-employed businesswoman. When I asked why American restaurants served such enormous helpings, she said, "Well, Americans still like to eat a lot; it's a way of building themselves up instead of relating to other people. Surrounding yourself with dishes is like drawing up the wagons."

This was her own observation; she had not read Philip Slater. I do not know if her comment was valid; nor, I suspect, does anyone. She herself lived on the fringes of a vigorous college community, and her comment may have reflected her marginal position; or it may have been a real insight into a harder business world than her academic friends knew. What I do know is that hers was a very American statement. She was not at all embarrassed to generalize about social-psychological attitudes. And she was concerned about the threat of acquisitive individualism to human fellowship. Her concern had a long history in American culture, as we shall see when we turn to the 'four fears.'

---

*The historian Allen F. Davis has suggested to me that for some professionals and executives, the 'summer place' (in Vermont or wherever) that stays in the family for generations provides a compensating community for bustling individualist lives.

5

Four Fears

(Part I)

My children are in elementary school and below, and all they care about, or what they care about most, is their lunchboxes today, their spelling test today and persuading me to buy them one more toy today. Tomorrow, let alone "moral purpose," isn't in their lexicon.

> Barbara T. Roessner, *Hartford Courant,*
> October 20, 1986[1]

We the people. They refute last week's television commentary downgrading our optimism and idealism. They are the entrepreneurs, the builders, the pioneers, and a lot of regular folks—the true heroes of our land who make up the most uncommon nation of doers in history. You know they're Americans because their spirit is as big as the universe, and their hearts are bigger than their spirit. . . .

America isn't finished; her best days have just begun.

> Ronald Reagan, State of the Union Address,
> January 27, 1987

The magnetic tension between individualism and community in America provides a field for the four fears. In exalting the freedoms of individualism, Americans frequently worry that they will lose them, will lose themselves to outside forces, will be owned and *want* to be owned—the sin of dependency. Yet Americans often fear the results of individualism: they worry that it makes them selfish and tears them apart.

Both fears aggravate the other fears. The fear of winding down, of losing vigor and momentum, draws at times from anxieties about losing self-reliance; at other times it draws from the very opposite, the belief that 'what's in it for me' undermines the social commitment, the sense of shared purpose, that gives dynamism to a community. And so it is not surprising that Americans often fear they are falling away from a past state of virtue and promise. Sometimes these fears arise spontaneously; sometimes they are invoked rhetorically, but even when they are, they usually strike chords in large numbers of people.

Although middle-class Americans have felt these fears about society as a whole, they have also applied them to their own lives—especially the fear of being owned and the fear of winding down. 'Are others controlling me too much?' 'Am I being induced to do things I shouldn't?' 'Am I doing as well as I should?' 'Have I lost a magic something I once had?' 'Is this all there is to life—what next?' These are common themes in the rich tapestry of American anxiousness, and indeed to some extent in the West generally.

This is not to deny that expansive optimism has been a keynote of American culture. One of the most intriguing aspects of the four fears is their coexistence with this optimism. Sometimes they have infiltrated it, so that bragging about the nation's future or one's own prospects becomes a whistling in the dark. At times, especially in recent years, optimism itself has been a measure of progress or decline: Let it be reported that Americans have become less hopeful about the nation's future, and immediately the fear of winding down gets to work, as writers and politicians suggest that America needs new frontiers, heroes, challenges. The very fact that the stock market depends on 'business confidence' makes a general mood—'bullishness' versus 'bearishness'—a yardstick of progress.

These assertions require some disclaimers. I do not claim that all periods and groups in America have been equally 'four-fearful'; that Americans have had no other characteristic fears; that the fears have been wholly irrational, unrelated to reality; or that only Americans have been privileged to have them. What is, or has been, particularly American is the recurrence of these fears through so much of the nation's history. I want to look at each of the fears in turn, and then see how they have appeared in different forms and combinations in different historical periods.

∗   ∗   ∗

The literary historian Stephen Fender has observed that a remarkable number of American best-sellers—from Mary Rowlandson's account of her Indian captivity (1670) through Kurt Vonnegut's *Slaughterhouse Five* (1970)—have been about capture, and that American war novels are often about capture or imprisonment by one's own side; a kind of double jeopardy. Another literary historian, Tony Tanner, has noticed in much of modern America's fiction the specter of total control and conditioning and the dream of unpatterned individualism.[2]

I see in all this the *fear of being owned.* I use the term 'owned' in a fairly wide range of senses. It includes the subjective condition of believing one is in some sense *enslaved.* It also includes the idea of *psychological* ownership by those who can manipulate one's identity. Indeed, as authority has become less brutal and more subtle, so the fear of *psychological* invasion has grown. Where other writers might simply use the word 'control,' I prefer 'ownership' because it resonates with the historic American drive to own property, which in turn sharpens the wish not to be owned *by* it—not to be controlled by the wealth of others or (a more upper-class sensibility) be too dependent on one's own possessions.

Enslavement by tyranny was, of course, a powerful image in the American Revolution and helped produce the Constitution's separation of powers. The idea is still strong today that America is a special nation of free persons, neither cowed by European class deference nor reduced to one gray plane by communism. The letters of nineteenth-century British immigrants making much of the wish to have no master are echoed in the longing of modern factory workers to 'be my own boss' or at least have the relative independence of a truck-driver or even a policeman. The historic American aversion to working as a domestic servant, a menial 'at someone's beck and call,' is of the same ilk.[3]

The conflict in American culture between the use of highly instructed organization to produce practical results and the idea of untrammeled independence has fomented the fear of being owned psychologically. The anxiety about becoming a compulsive 'yes-man,' which helped produce William Whyte's market in the 1950s, showed up again in Michael Maccoby's study of high-tech managers in the early 1970s. More than half of them worried that they gave in too much to others. Small wonder that popular therapists have written best sellers telling readers how to deal with browbeaters, stop apologizing, and start "pulling your own strings."[4]

In job terms, one apparent solution to the fear of being owned is to be an owner, to go to work for oneself—if and when one can afford to. In 1986, the twenty-fifth anniversary year of my Harvard class, I estimated that the self-employed proportion of the class had quadrupled over the previous fifteen years, from about 4 percent to around 16 percent. Many of these had started out in organizations but switched when they felt they could. To their number we could add a further 18 percent or so who had already chosen the considerable autonomy of being a college professor.

One response, indeed, to the fear of being owned is to be a highly qualified professional. As an ambitious working-class youth put it, "I want to get enough knowledge so nobody can tell me what to do."[5] For some, however, the guild rules and requirements of being a doctor or lawyer seem to fence in the free spirit. And so behold, in almost every branch of the economy, the free-lance *consultant,* riding in to sell 'hands-on' wisdom without necessarily having years of formal training or sticking around to see the job completed.

The fear of being owned also appears in feminism, and nowhere in the West has feminism been stronger than in the United States. In imitating the Declaration of Independence, the Seneca Falls Declaration of Sentiments of 1848 implied that Americans had a special responsibility to ensure rights and liberties for women. The 1848 Declaration virtually accused men of owning women. Man's "absolute despotism" usurped women's property and deprived women of opportunity; it made married women "civilly dead." Man's "tyranny" also threatened a woman's character: it sought to "destroy her confidence in her own powers, to lessen her self-respect, and to make herself willing to lead a dependent and abject life."

This psychological element, which the Declaration only touched upon, has been greatly expanded in the modern women's movement. Whereas educated women in the late nineteenth and early twentieth centuries often resisted male mastery by staying single, more women now want to fight it closer in. They provide a market for the kind of psychotactical manual that tells women how to stand up, inwardly as well as outwardly, to the men they live and work with. The ultimate issue, again, is one of psychological ownership: Who is to determine a woman's identity—what she is valued for, how she behaves, and how she sees herself?[6]

Such books have their uses: They are one of the more valid off-shoots of 'assertiveness training,' which became such a vogue in the 1970s. Nevertheless, they are part of a popular literature that plays down interdependence. In proclaiming that people can remake themselves, in treating their social past as an enemy, and in focusing on a sovereign self, the 'how-to' books of psychic independence represent the atomizing tendency in American life so decried by the social-character books of the seventies and early eighties. Indeed, the first type of book, addressed to the fear of being owned, has been a goad to the second type of book, expressing the *fear of falling apart*.[7]

That fear, to be sure, is alive and well, too, in popular manuals of healthy living. There are any number of anecdotal tracts on the importance of reaching out and 'touching' others; they have even penetrated the literature of business success.[8] But the fear of falling apart extends much further than this; it has a wider base than worries about the divisive effects of 'Reagan capitalism' or the legacies of the "Me Decade." Arthur M. Schlesinger, Jr., said much about the fear when he explained in large historical terms the political caution of President Kennedy. "Its basic source," he suggested, was

> an acute and anguished sense of the fragility of the membranes of civilization, stretched so thin over a nation so disparate in its composition, so tense in its interior relationships, so cunningly enmeshed in underground fears and antagonisms, so entrapped by history in the ethos of violence.[9]

Schlesinger was influenced by Kennedy's civil rights problems and his fear of pushing the white South too far, a South that conjured up sectional anarchy, the nightmare of the Civil War. But the problem is not just historical. No heavily industrialized country has higher murder rates than the United States; and none has a greater contrast between a large rural population (still more than a quarter of the whole) and huge metropolitan areas. How quickly one can move in America from a sense of being uniformly shaped by a bland and comfortable commerce to a sense of losing touch in a jungle of impersonal freeways and desolate inner cities!

The undertone of impending threat in all this is well caught by Judy Blume's formula stories of the 1970s and '80s for young teenage girls. A lively, warmhearted heroine lives on a nice, middle-class block, but around her, and sometimes within her, there is a more frightening world of change. Violence may strike, or racist ugliness, or even just a move to a new neighborhood and school—all on top of the inner strain of growing up, wanting to be 'developed' while feeling a child.

Though much of this is not new, the long-term rise in divorces and the more recent surge in the number of persons living alone have probably brought the sensation of falling apart closer to more people. In December 1986, the columnist Ellen Goodman wrote about Thanksgiving Day entirely in this vein. She described the gathering together of families as "rituals of intimacy" for Americans who lived apart and felt alone. Thanksgiving answered basic needs for community, clanship, and a shared home. It affirmed, likewise, a "sense of oneness" between generations. Americans had to *choose* whether to 'go home' in this way, but they obeyed a powerful longing when they did.[10]

I mention Goodman's piece not just for what it said but because she felt it worth saying to her widespread audience at such length, and in such a tone of mournful celebration. I note particularly her view of tradition as a "special glue [that holds] us together over time" as well as "distance." Just as Christopher Lasch feared that Americans had isolated themselves in the present, so other writers have yearned for the opposite. In the preface to his *History of the American People* (1984), Stephan Thernstrom hoped that readers would "gain a greater measure of self-understanding and a stronger sense of connection with their ancestors, a new feeling for what Abraham Lincoln called 'the mystic chords of memory' that tie successive generations of America together." This statement was not penned by a zealous civics teacher or a romantic nationalist, but by a Harvard professor who had made his name in statistical studies of ethnic groups, social class, and mobility.

Thernstrom's statement was characteristically American. It appealed first to an individualist desire for self-knowledge and then to a wish for social roots and a sense of relatedness.[11] A similar dualism appears in the American middle-class habit of using a family middle name or initial, or giving one's son the same name and tacking on 'Junior.' (Were he a Briton or an Australian, Arthur Schlesinger would never be referred to as Arthur M. Schlesinger, Jr. What titles he might have collected is another matter.) These American styles inflate the individual name while connecting it to generations of family.

If the past is seen (sometimes wistfully) as a source of connection, it is also viewed anxiously as a baseline of achievement. The *fear of winding down* is sharpened by the traditional belief that Americans are a people of energy and reach, forever scaling new heights. The "go-aheadativeness" of American businessmen, as the *New York Times* called it in 1855, is supposed to contrast with the hidebound, class-bound inhibitions of older, European societies. When Studs Terkel interviewed successful business people in the 1970s for his book *American Dreams: Lost and Found,* several of them proclaimed a social Darwinist law of competition and survival: "if you don't go up, you go down. Nothing ever stays the same. You get bigger and better, or you go the other way."[12]

The fear of 'going the other way' is particularly pronounced in the "active-negative" character who drives himself to do more than he really wants to. Richard Nixon wrote of his life as a series of crisis tests whose main danger came afterward—letting his guard drop and making mistakes "when the body, mind and spirit [were] totally exhausted." The same either/or attitude popped up when Nixon spoke of being a Wall Street lawyer. New York was "a place where you can't slow down—a fast track. Any person tends to vegetate unless he is moving on a fast track."[13]

A similar concern ran through the Cold War classic *The Ugly American,* by William Lederer and Eugene Burdick (1958), a best-selling medley of cautionary tales, which helped instigate the Peace Corps. In their operations against communism in the Far East, the American protagonists have to be alert at all times, for at any moment the most competent hero may be sapped, seduced, or bamboozled by cunning enemies deploying a sophisticated, old-world culture.[14]

The fear of winding down draws on two personal anxieties: the fear of failure when society makes life a race and tags 'also rans' as losers; and a worry about losing vigor, competence, and the ability to gain from new experiences. It provides a market for books like Srully Blotnick's *The Corporate Steeplechase* (1984), which warns readers that they may falter at any point—even by alienating others—and then tells them how to deal with these reassuringly "predictable crises." (As in Nixon's case, the fear of winding down can also be a fear of falling apart, of failure through uncontrolled aggressiveness.) Manuals on how to live also tell Americans—as if they need to be told!—that setbacks are "necessary losses," which can lead to "growth." High career success can have a 'downside'—depression, for instance, or isolation—but take heart: this can be avoided. Material success must also be emotional success.[15]

This play with images of failure may, in part, reflect the language of decline and loss which has been so energetically applied to the country as a whole since the Vietnam defeat and the slide in America's industrial competitiveness. It was against this language that Ronald Reagan cast his rhetoric, affirming "there are no limits to growth . . . when men and women are free to follow their dreams."[16] Throughout the nation's history, however, commentators have lamented the loss of one or another key to American vigor and momentum: republican frugality, smallholder democracy, 'free land' and the frontier, WASP supremacy, and technological edge (viz., the sputnik scare of the fifties).

In the twentieth century, one source of worry about winding down has been, again, the paradox of organization. Americans have looked to large-scale, corporate bureaucracy for collective effectiveness, yet within that bureaucracy the clerk and even the middle manager can easily feel *in*effective, unimportant, and stuck in a rut. One's location may vault from Connecticut to California, but does the job really change? To allay such doubts there is the executive 'motivation' industry (where one series of conferences has called itself American Renewal). Admittedly, the problem has become more pressing in recent years. As business growth slackens and the baby-boomers crowd into middle management, more of them are going to feel what one shrewd author-therapist has christened "the plateauing trap"—the suspicion that your last promotion lies behind you and no breaks lie ahead.[17] This is only a problem, however, in a society where 'onward and upward' is supposed to be the norm; where 'steady state' equals 'failure,' even when it means doing an old job well.

The fear of winding down is not confined to careers and organizations. One appeal of the born-again Christian idea is to make each day fresh and full and significant by living it in Christ's service. When the religious beliefs fit, this is especially important for the middle-class housewife, who is apt to feel a sense of loss and decline sooner than her husband. She is, after all, taught that homemaking is not a real job, that raising children and cultivating interests within and without the home are not worthy of a college education—and when her children are older and she does get into the job market, it is easy to feel left behind by younger women who got there first, not to speak of all the better-paid men.

Then again there is the matter of consumer affluence, which has unsettled so many middle-class Americans. It has made them guilty about waste and flabbiness, while giving them the means and space to go jogging or hit the Jane Fonda workout trail. The natural decline of aging must be resisted. You may joke about it ad nauseam, and if you are a writer you may publish self-piteous confessions about 'mid-life crisis,' about horizons closing in, and about the way young people regard you. What you must not do is simply accept it.[18] Meanwhile, for the nation as a whole, there is always the President's Council on Physical Fitness. From its founding by Eisenhower, it has issued periodic and well-publicized alarms about national physical decline.[19] Jogging and Jane Fonda, it seems, are no match in the general populace for junk food and television.*

In his history of American physical-fitness cults, Harvey Green argues that they started in the anxious individualism of the 1830s. When the social fabric seemed to be disintegrating, some people turned to their bodies for perfection. Whether or not this is true, the fear of personal and physical decline has sometimes involved a moral anxiety for the whole nation, a *fear of falling away* from the standards and commandments of the past.[20]

In the rhetoric of the Moral Majority's Reverend Jerry Falwell, the fear of falling away summons the other fears too. Weakened by a "tide of permissiveness and moral decay," Americans have lost the will to work and strive that built the nation (enter the fear of winding down). "Purposeless" and adrift, without common values (the fear of falling

---

*The physical-fitness reports have often focused on the young, and the fear of winding down is no monopoly of 'mature' citizens. The ebullient sixteen-year-old daughter of a college professor told me that of the four fears I mentioned, her biggest fear was of winding down. She didn't so much fear being owned, she said: she was confident she could "play along" with any organization and still be "my own person." But she did worry sometimes about "getting sluggish" and "slowing down." She seemed to me to be the opposite of these things, spreading her life between studying for college, working in a pizza restaurant, and singing in a band—for which, she said, she needed to stay "looking young."

apart), Americans have been taken over by "welfarism" and made vulnerable to communist domination (the fear of being owned).[21]

Admittedly, the fear of moral and social decline from a past, better state is not uniquely American. What is more distinctively American is the double idea of failing a past standard of basic character *and* a past commission to build on that character: to fulfill it and, more than fulfill it, to *progress*. (According to a national survey in 1985, a plurality of Americans in widely differing groups—old, young, rich, poor, labor union, southern white—considered 'progressive' to be a favorable description of a public figure. No such support was won by 'liberal,' 'conservative,' 'populist,' or even 'moderate.'[22]) Just as the immigrant's child must surpass his or her parents in knowledge and ability, must realize and go beyond the dreams for which they struggled, so Americans must keep faith with a national promise that is demanding yet open-ended. They must retain the virtue of their ancestors, but they must also do more with it, to satisfy and enlarge the human spirit. Fulfilling their own history, they must resist the history of other great nations: national ascendancy must not be followed by decline.

I do not say that most middle-class Americans consciously tell themselves all this. Nonetheless, the fear of falling away affects them, for it runs through the culture, surfacing in countless campaign speeches and valedictorian addresses. In its celebration of change and progress it is an exciting burden, but a burden it remains, for at any time Rocket America may—according to one standpoint—take a false bearing. Indeed, the very industriousness and energy of the nation can betray it (here the fear of winding down diverges from the fear of falling away) or deplete it so that the people lose both vigor and virtue. "Will you tell me," wrote John Adams in 1819, "how to prevent riches becoming the effects of temperance and industry? Will you tell me how to prevent riches from producing luxury? Will you tell me how to prevent luxury from producing effeminacy, intoxication, extravagance, vice and folly?"[23] Campaigning in 1960 against the fat privatism of the Eisenhower years, Senator John F. Kennedy shared some of Adams's doubts.

> The very abundance which our dynamism has created has weaned and wooed us from the tough condition in which, hencetofore, we have approached whatever it is we have had to do. A man who has

extra fat will look doubtfully on attempting the four-minute mile; a nation, replete with goods and services, confident that "there's more where that came from," may feel less ardor for questing.[24]

The notion of America as a special ark of Providence—defender of freedom and shining light of progress—creates anxiety as well as hope. When John Winthrop uttered the famous words in his shipboard sermon of 1630, "we shall be as a city upon a hill, the eyes of all people are upon us," he added the swift negative, "so that if we shall deal falsely with our god in this work we have undertaken and so cause him to withdraw his present help from us, we shall be made a story and a by-word through the world . . . ."[25] It is true that Winthrop and the earliest Puritan settlers had a particular sense of being watched, by Europe as well as by God. But that sense never died, and since America has become a world power, the idea of being on show and test before the world has revived. The fear of failure before an audience is obviously more secular than in Winthrop's version, but the shift is only relative: the idea remains both religious and political.[26]

The idea of falling away does not always point to a particular generation that has set the standard for its successors. For some people there is just a sense of decline from 'how things used to be.' Nor is there total agreement among those who do refer to a specific set of forebears. Some refer to their parents' or grandparents' generation; others are more likely to summon a mid-nineteenth-century picture, of frontier settlers, perhaps, or of Victorian entrepreneurs. The most common public references, however, are to the era of the Founding Fathers and the first few decades of the Republic.[27]

The boundaries of this period are vague to most of its venerators (sometimes they include the early Jacksonian years), but its images give a distinctively American flavor to the fear of falling away. Its hold on the imagination stems most obviously from the Revolution itself, with its legends of patriotic sacrifice; from the creation of a 'living Constitution'; from the hallowed status of its signatories (especially Washington and Jefferson), meeting together in fertile debate; and from the rhetoric of liberty that ran through those events.

The rights and goals announced in the Declaration of Independence and the preamble to the Constitution could not be perfectly fulfilled. They would always, therefore, be a challenge to future generations to improve on the past. At the same time, for modern intellectuals unhappy about contemporary trends—a Whyte infuriated by conformity, a Bellah distressed by privatism—the early Republic appears to have reached a better balance of citizenship and individualism. An era when voluntary associations really did proliferate, it also seemed to be a time when most people stood on their own feet and were producers, not manipulators.[28]

Speeches by Presidents and presidential candidates have often invoked the Revolutionary-Constitutional era in seeking redemption of the Republic—redemption their way. Franklin Roosevelt used it in 1936 to attack usurpations by big business ("economic royalists": see page 103). Richard Nixon used it in 1968 to attack usurpations by big government.[29] But the fullest use of it in a famous modern speech was Martin Luther King's address ("I have a dream") at the civil rights March on Washington in 1963.

King combined a language of republican democracy with respectable metaphors of business finance. "The architects of our republic" had signed "a promissory note . . . of life, liberty and the pursuit of happiness . . . to which every American was to fall heir." America had "defaulted on this promissory note"; it had "given the Negro people a bad check." In calling for justice, King invited Americans to look forward as well as back, to make America a "great nation," transforming its "jangling discords" into a "beautiful symphony of brotherhood." In this way King used and then assuaged the nation's fear of falling apart in racial strife. But he also deployed a fear of falling away, challenging the country to "rise up and live out the full meaning of its creed," the Declaration of Independence.[30]

> I have a dream that one day every valley shall be exalted, every hill and mountain shall be made low, the rough places will be made plain, and the crooked places will be made straight, and the glory of the Lord shall be revealed, and all flesh shall see it together . . .
>
> From every mountainside, let freedom ring.

Toward the end of his speech, the Reverend King repaired to nature—first in biblical idiom and then in language closer to that of presidential candidates, invoking the range and majesty of the American continent. From "the snow-capped Rockies of Colorado" to "Lookout Mountain of Tennessee," he summoned a geographical *e pluribus unum*.[31]

At the heart of what Americans have often been afraid of losing is just this, a state of nature: a nourishing, stabilizing essential for all future growth. The central fear is that of falling away, but the others are involved also. To lose naturalness is to lose a source of vigor as well as virtue; and the artifice that controls and manipulates people may also sunder natural ties.

The Puritan settlers, it is true, were ambivalent to nature. If sin, in their eyes, often came through the vices of unnatural living, it also came through natural pride, which should be curbed at an early age. Looking outward too, the colonial Puritans, and indeed many nineteenth-century settlers, viewed the wilderness as a place of desolation and degeneracy, to be resisted or conquered rather than embraced.

Yet colonial Americans also bequeathed to the Revolution and the early Republic an idea of the New World as a preserve of benign liberty, innocent of the artificial corruptions and oppressions of Europe. Nature's gentleman, a plain-living, plain-dealing homesteader, unaffected by fancy ranks and hierarchies, became an American ideal. As it traveled through the nineteeth century, the ideal remained essentially pastoral, but it was quickened by the more assertive qualities associated with frontiersmen.[32]

Two problems remained. How on earth could one go on thinking of America itself as especially natural when its success was increasingly bound up with machines? And how could Americans keep their natural, sturdy innocence in a sophisticated modern society?

As Leo Marx, the literary historian, has suggested, one way of jibing technology with nature was to smooth the former into the latter, to see machinery as an extension—an exciting extension—of nature's power. When Daniel Webster inaugurated the opening of the Northern Railroad to Grafton, New Hampshire, in 1847, he did not simply debunk the opposition, though he did that too. Where he might have spoken of rails, he used instead the gentler image of steam. He presented the railroad as part of a natural progress. Local residents, himself included, had already experienced that progress when rough and tedious country roads had given way to turnpike and canal. The railroad, he implied, was no fiercer than the rugged mountains and gorges which it "threaded." It brought friends together from afar, and for the occasion could even bring them fresh fish from the sea![33]

At the end of the nineteenth century, Frederick Jackson Turner suggested another way of joining nature to technological progress.

Like a giant reaper advancing up a slope, its blades revolving back toward the earth, "American development" did not move on one plane but returned

> to primitive conditions on a continually advancing frontier line, and a new development for that area . . . This perennial rebirth . . . this expansion westward with its new opportunities, its continuous touch with the simplicity of primitive society, furnish the forces dominating American character.

In modern American political rhetoric, the language of 'rebirth' and 'regeneration' has long been a staple. Turner did not invent it, as he himself recognized, but he showed its connection with a mystique of nature.[34]

In tenuous forms, both the Webster and the Turner images have survived into our own time. Webster's notion appears in the idea of 'harnessing the elements' (the hydroelectric dam) and in designs that follow nature (the aerodynamic shape). Turner's vision recurs in back-to-nature movements and the hoary assumption that country boys may still be needed to preserve democracy, purify modern life, and deliver an invigorating comeuppance to city slickers. From Jimmy Carter's 1976 campaign (Georgia boy takes Washington) to the movie *Crocodile Dundee* (Aussie takes New York), these romantic notions live on.[35]

But symbolism is not enough. There remains a deep anxiety about the 'phony' (a word that has no exact equivalent in British English). It is an old question: How does nature's gentleman keep his integrity when success is so tied up with salesmanship, including *self*-salesmanship, the art of 'projecting personality'—when indeed, in politics at least, the 'country boy' often turns out to be an affectation?

Well before the Civil War, as the historian Karen Haltunen has shown, middle-class advice literature was warning its readers of the danger of the confidence man, luring innocent youth into vice or financial ruin. Such fears were to be expected in an exploding commercial society where almost anyone you met was more and more likely to be a stranger.[36] As marketing became more organized in the late nineteenth century, sincerity remained an anxiously valued quality, both for selling goods and for resisting the salesman's influence. In *The Virginian* (1902), Owen Wister anticipated a generation of 'plastic society'-haters when he scorned the traveling salesman's "being too soon with everybody, the celluloid good-fellowship that passes for ivory with nine in ten of the city crowd. But not so with the sons of the sage-brush. They live nearer nature, and they know better." Rededicating his book to Theodore Roosevelt nine years later, Wister hailed him for starting to restore to public life "the lost habit of sincerity"; it was needed, Wister said, to hold the nation together through the industrial conflicts fomented by Wall Street.[37]

Four decades later, in *The Lonely Crowd,* David Riesman et al. observed a frustrated American yearning for sincerity and authentic craftsmanship, against the "false personalization" of white-collar work.[38] Again, one of the issues in Joe McGinniss's widely read book, *The Selling of the President 1968,* was whether the presentation of Richard Nixon in TV spots and panel shows created a false image of the candidate or revealed a truer aspect of him than the anti-Nixon biases of newspapermen had let through. The ambiguity of it all showed up in the character of Nixon's advertising director, Harry Treleaven. Raised a Christian Scientist (no artificial medicines till he was twenty-one), he appreciated old things like whaling ships, admired the British for their seemingly effortless style, and was fascinated with the craft of making artificial flowers look natural. What did he really want: to be natural, or just to look it?[39]

The problem, then, was not just artificiality but imitations of the natural—a counterfeiting of the authentic or spontaneous—which affronted the historic American sense of being 'genuine,' 'just folks.' One of the sources of Ronald Reagan's popularity was his manner of friendly genuineness. In this regard, his well-known bloopers probably helped—until 'Irangate.' Yet for many intellectuals, outside Middle America, and long before Irangate, his popularity seemed mainly based on a skill at communicating: the 'Teflon President—nothing sticks'—was a movie-made persona. Even the familiar wag of the head was thought to be contrived. As a modern Owen Wister might have warned, American friendliness, that famous national warmth, could be the pseudofriendliness of customer relations.[40]

When Christopher Lasch, writing in the late 1970s, called America a "hall of mirrors," where show and reality blurred, he himself was refracting *The Image,* Daniel Boorstin's book of 1962, which described America as a "wall of mirrors." Initially subtitled *or What Happened to the American Dream,* Boorstin's work enjoyed a new attention from intellectuals in the late seventies and early eighties.[41] It described a modern society of fake candor and commercially packaged experience. America's special dreams and aspirations had given way to passive illusions, its moral heroes to celebrities, its notions of virtue to the business of making a good impression. Hurling snippets of knowledge and entertainment together, the media at once disintegrated and homogenized experience and so controlled it. Boorstin presented an America invaded and corrupted by artificiality: he expressed in subtle ways the fears of being owned and falling apart, as well as the fears of winding down and falling away.*

---

*In a rather beautiful passage of religious summons, Boorstin concluded by calling Americans back to the voyage of real "discovery" for which "the New World gave us a grand, unique beginning." His solution was personal understanding and honesty, not political action or planned institutional change. He blamed no capitalist system or class for what Americans, and other modern peoples, were letting happen.[42]

6

Four Fears

(Part II)

You have better food and raiment than was in former times: but
have you better hearts than your forefathers had? If so, rejoice in
that mercy, and let New-England then shout for joy. Sure, all the
people of God in other parts of the world, that shall hear that the
children and grand-children of the first planters have better hearts
and are more heavenly than their predecessors, they will doubtless
greatly rejoice, and will say, "This is the generation whom the Lord
hath blessed."

The Memoirs of Capt. Roger Clapp, Boston, c. 1680[1]

The condition of the people can never remain stationary. When not
improving they are sinking deeper and deeper into slavery. Eternal
vigilance alone can sustain them, and never ceasing exertion is
necessary for their social and political improvement.

Frederick Robinson, July 4 speech to
Boston Trades Union, 1834[2]

To convey in one chapter the full reach of the four fears through
American history is impossible. I can only pick out some of the more
visible and public ways in which they have come together. Let me
begin with an extreme phenomenon—the attraction of diverse groups
in America to conspiracy theories, from eighteenth-century suspicions of British and Jacobin plots to recent specters of communist
subversion.

In many of these fevers, the seemingly opposite fears of falling apart
and being owned unite in one theme: the idea that an un-American

force is sowing anarchy in order to pull down established authority and gain control over people's minds and lives. Belief in a hostile conspiracy offers a way of drawing people together against a threat to American liberty and progress. It also supplies a scapegoat when the society itself seems to be failing. The fear of falling away from a special American promise turns some groups into decontamination squads, ferreting out the agents of Toryism, Rome, Jewish bankers, the Kremlin, etc., who threaten to drag America down.

On a personal plane, the strains of individualism cause a fear of being owned, which in turn may produce conspiracy theories. The sequence may go like this: 'I am supposed to be in total control of my life. I am *not* in control of it. Therefore illegitimate forces are controlling me.' Here political facts may assist fantasy. Because traditions of freedom have restricted American government and sliced it up into 'separate powers,' informal networks of influence have had to be evolved to get things done. These networks invite rumors of secret plots. Of course, such plots do occur, as everyone since Watergate knows; but American conspiracy theories have usually involved alien, or partly alien, forces, whose scheming influence they have grotesquely exaggerated.[3]

Three of the four fears in American history go all the way back to seventeenth-century Puritanism. (The fear of winding down did not really get going till after the Revolution, at least not in public form.) We have already noted John Winthrop's sense of being on test before God and the world as he and his company set about building their community on the Massachusetts shore. For Winthrop, the danger of falling away from God's "special commission" was inseparable from the urgency of holding together, in abundance as in hardship: of caring for each other, of devoting private wealth to generosity rather than to materialist ambition, of making class differences themselves a source of mutual obligation.[4]

These concerns continued through the history of colonial New England Puritanism. Productive work was admired and the enjoyment of rewards accepted, but luxuries and moneymaking were always viewed anxiously as a potential distraction from God's community. Yet more and more people resisted church control and insisted on living their own lives, economically and spiritually. Some, like Anne Hutchinson, used the church's own tradition of nonconformism based on personal religious experience to reject almost all church authority in matters of worship. They made the fear of being owned into a religious principle.

All this fed the worry of clergymen and their followers about the "declension" of their new Israel from the Bible's special charge to them and from the supposed virtue and simplicity of the founding settlers. The fear of backsliding was intensified by the Calvinist doctrine of grace, according to which you could never know for sure that you had been saved. If you did think you knew it, you approached the deadly sin of pride. In response to these tensions there soon emerged in Massachusetts and elsewhere the election-sermon jeremiad. Addressing the new legislature on election day, a festive occasion of new arrival and coming together, a minister would review the spiritual state of the commonwealth. Frequently he would scold his audience for falling away and falling apart, for failing the sacred opportunities given them. In doing so he looked gloomily backward, but he also looked forward, with a glint of hope.[5]

By the 1770s, election sermons had joined the rhetoric of Revolution. As the idea of New World virtue against Old World corruption and oppression acquired a new political edge, it seemed as urgent as ever to warn the people against moral backsliding. When colonists boycotted British consumer goods, the Puritan concept of frugality (an ideal that went back to the Roman moralists) became part of the newly emerging national consciousness. Making and wearing homespun was at once an economic weapon and a collective symbol.[6]

The fear of falling away thus entered and helped shape the Revolution. So did the fears of being owned and falling apart, and these two fears permeated each other in new ways. Bernard Bailyn has demonstrated that Revolutionary pamphleteers inherited a view of power and liberty developed by seventeenth-century English radicals. In this view, the weakness and lusts of human nature made power forever aggressive, liberty fragile, and the people vulnerable to enslavement. On top of this, the presence of black slavery made Revolutionary Americans especially sensitive to despotism in everyday life.

Tyranny, however, was also seditious. As Stephen Fender has shown, the Declaration of Independence married its assault on royal tyranny to an English Tory tradition of satire against factional dissension. The British king, it declared, had "excited domestic insurrections amongst us," exposed the state to internal "convulsions," and frustrated the enactment of urgent laws.[7]

Conversely, sedition was tyrannical. The Constitution itself reflected the belief that factionalism and popular 'passions'—in a sense, too much democracy—could, unless checked, produce a tyranny of the majority, or what George Washington, in his Farewell Address, later called a "frightful despotism": the "alternate domination of one [vengeful] faction over another." Washington's idea of faction in that speech was largely regional (North versus South, East versus West), whereas Jefferson's idea of "insurrections," as he meant it in the Declaration, was largely racial. Both men, though, were of their time in sharing another belief: that a person could be enslaved by his own lusts and weaknesses. It was a belief that was at once Puritan and eighteenth-century rationalist.[8]

Anxieties like these lasted long after the Revolution. As they had done in the Revolutionary period itself, political moralists referred to an earlier republic, recalling a ghastly Roman trajectory from simple-living patriotism to selfish dissipation. Luxury, still associated with European imports, seemed divisive and enervating. It was a cultural Trojan horse, inviting the weak and flighty to denature and de-Americanize themselves in spurious imitations of European styles. It was also a real source of the post-Revolution slump, when imports dangerously exceeded exports. Despite the hardships of that depression, moral watchmen were soon warning of the dangers of sinking into comfortable pursuits, by contrast with the vigorous wartime fellowship of the Revolution. The fear of falling apart thus gathered to it the fear of winding down.

From this standpoint, the nation's economic development could mean personal degeneration. Too much commerce, too much consumption, would produce both greed and dependence. For a Jefferson, it took time to adjust from a purely agrarian ideal to admitting that a little investment in industry might actually help to create happier and more enlightened citizens by raising living standards. Others had long been fired with the notion of technical and business progress, but the belief persisted well into the 1830s that a rural setting was the best moral environment for a factory work force.[9]

This attitude was not confined to Americans. In England too, early textile manufacturers often wanted to avoid the slum conditions of Manchester, which had become a blackened, proletarian city by the late eighteenth century. But because America's industrial development came later than Britain's, Manchester for Americans was more a specter from the *past,* the symbol of degenerate order.[10]

The year 1832 marked the centenary of George Washington's birth and the death of Charles Carroll, last surviving signer of the Declaration of Independence. The party system was re-forming, and as a new breed of political manager moved to the fore, commentators anxiously compared their own generation with that of the Founding Fathers. Michael Kammen has observed that throughout the 1830s, '40s, and '50s, in North and South alike, two questions recurred in speeches and odes: "Are we worthy of our revolutionary forebears? Are we undoing, by our divisiveness, all that they worked so hard to obtain?"[11] For an educated, articulate minority, especially clergymen in the 1840s and '50s, the very pace of America's growth was dangerous, threatening to whirl it apart into chaos. Self-indulgent materialism remained the traditional target, but the growth of economic inequality also encouraged the fear of urban mob turbulence and, less frequently, an upbraiding of the rich for neglecting the poor.[12]

In this period, then, the fear of falling away was entwined as closely as ever with the fear of falling apart. The fear of winding down was less obvious, but it appeared too, in conjunction with the other fears. Frederick Robinson's remarks quoted at the head of this chapter, about the need for popular vigilance against "sinking," were part of an assault on monopoly by left-wing Democrats. Robinson implicitly rejected the assumption that free land and economic growth would automatically provide gains for everyone. Enrichment of "the thousands [was] always contrary to the interests of the millions." To prevent their enslavement by "the aristocracy," the people should wake up and regain the rights their fathers had won for them. Robinson was pleased that the people were "beginning to bestir themselves"; like so many exponents of the four fears, he hedged his criticism with hope.[13]

The theme of enslavement also joined with the fear of winding down in the high-powered temperance movements of the period.

Taking "ardent spirits," reformers stressed, would not only debilitate the drinker and destroy his home; it would make him a "captive," in "cruel bondage" as surely as was the black slave. In the free-enterprise culture of the North, the fear of being owned and controlled—either personally or by remote monopolies and conspiracies—supplied a special overtone to political debate.[14]

This is not to deny that expansive optimism lay at the heart of Jacksonian middle-class attitudes. Yet the young Abraham Lincoln was not alone in combining ambition with what he and others called "hypo" (depressive hypochondria). A fear of failure may well have contributed to this. On a public plane, even nationalist celebrants could "Rejoice with Trembling," as one divine had urged them to do.[15] A rich example at midcentury was the Fourth of July speech given by another rising young lawyer, William Arthur, at Covington, Kentucky. Like earlier commentators, Arthur believed that America, growing ever greater, could break free from the usual cycles of national rise and decline. Seeking "limitless expanse" and "burning with generous rivalry," the American was "the annointed civiliser, the only visible source of light and heat to the dark and discordant and troubled world." Yet "eternal vigilance" was needed, for if Americans fell away by one iota from the guiding spirit of the Constitution, they would lose their liberties and be ridiculed by mankind. As Sacvan Bercovitch has pointed out, this warning—like Winthrop's but with more stress on liberty—was a refrain of many speeches in the 1830s and '40s.[16]

Even the optimistic creed of Manifest Destiny, the belief that God and natural law required America to extend its special blessings and liberties across the whole continent and maybe beyond—even this doctrine was tinctured by the four fears. Expansionists sometimes justified their policy as a way of preventing European encroachment and "domination." It was, in other words, a safeguard against falling away into the colonial ignominy of being controlled by another power. Some expansionists also worried that the nation might fall apart into race and class conflict and wind down into economic depression. Gaining new land and markets in California, in Texas, and farther south would provide resettlement zones for blacks and urban workers, and new customers to keep up farm prices.[17]

But opponents of expansion, too, could refer to falling away and falling apart. In opposing those who would annex Texas by supporting its revolt against Mexico, the Unitarian minister and writer William Ellery Channing declared that support of such a revolution "contaminated our own." Taking Texas would "add a new career of crime" to a country already corrupted by prosperity, where "moral independence" had yielded to greed and ostentation—to "anxious, envious, discontented strivings." By giving new territory to the slave states, furthermore, it would inflame and extend the slavery issue and so "endanger the Union." On this last point at least, Channing's fear of falling apart was realistic and prescient.[18]

In no political history were the four fears more decisive than in the causes of the Civil War. On both sides, all four fears supplied a set of holy hatreds that escalated the dispute over slavery versus 'free soil' in the new western territories; they moved that dispute from economic and political contest to violent disunion. Even the fear of falling apart became, under the influence of the other fears, an agent of sectional distrust rather than national unity. Each side accused the other of trying to dominate it through turbulence. Each shrilly exaggerated its own class cohesion and imputed exploitation to the other.

By the 1850s, northerners had a picture of the South that drew on Revolutionary and early republican specters of Europe. The South, in this view, was a contaminating civilization build around an oppressive aristocracy. 'The Slave Power' did not just enslave blacks; it degraded ordinary whites and aggressively threatened 'free institutions' throughout the United States. 'The Slave Power' had dragged down its own society, producing a stagnant economy, a degenerate populace, and a mayhem of brutal customs—quarreling, dueling, lynching (here antislavery propagandists dumped on the South more widespread frontier practices).

While some martial moralists in the Northeast feared that southern chivalry would produce better fighters than would Yankee commercialism, it was also thought that slave labor would artificially undercut 'free labor' in the western territories. In the attitude of Free-Soilers, the Dred Scott decision, forbidding Congress to ban slavery in the territories, was itself a restrictive abstraction, concocted by an elderly Chief Justice in his "slippered leisure" (as the *New York Herald* put it), while muscular tradesmen and farmers of the North were following a "law of nature" in moving west and "elbowing the slaves further south." In the higher-toned view of Abraham Lincoln, the march of slavery into the territories had violated the equal-rights humanity of the Declaration of Independence and "the principles of progress" for which the world looked to the United States.[19]

For the South's defenders, these attitudes were an aggressive betrayal of the Founders—the Constitution, after all, had recognized slavery—but what else could one expect from a hypocritical business system where jumped-up plutocrats exploited their wage labor and practiced a cold and anarchic individualism? The South, by contrast, was a garden of virtue where the planters took personal responsibility for their slaves and their communities. Abolish slavery and one would get, in the words of John Calhoun, "poverty, desolation and wretchedness."

Southern ideologues, in fact, grossly exaggerated the popularity of abolitionism in the North and the danger of slave revolts instigated by northern subversives. In their mounting paranoia, southern spokesmen used Revolutionary images of 'enslavement' by a corrupt, and corrupting, North. Their comparison between southern slavery and a 'greater' enslaving impulse in the North seemed, at times, to project onto the North their own guilt about owning slaves while espousing freedom for themselves.

What leaders of both sections did agree upon was that slavery must 'expand or die'—move into new land or eventually wither. Economic historians are not so unanimous today about the truth of this, but the proposition was so generally *assumed* to be true at the time that it suggests the influence of a more basic concept of winding down: the belief that if a system did not advance it would decline. Politically, the wish to expand terrain on both sides was inflamed by an exaggerated idea of the disaster that would ensue if the other side gained a lasting preponderance in Congress. And psychologically, for southern leaders, it was intolerable that their system should be *contained,* should be held from sharing in America's Manifest Destiny.[20]

In his July 4 oration of 1876, the country's most famous minister, Henry Ward Beecher, looked back to slavery and found the nation redeemed—educated by that great issue and regenerated by the war. Fixing his gaze gratefully but boldly on the nation's "fathers," he declared that contemporary Americans had more than justified their handiwork and virtues. "We often mope and vex ourselves with melancholy prognostications concerning this or that danger"—

a trait inherited "from our ancestors"—but the truth was that Americans had gone far beyond them, in enlightenment as well as quality of life.[21]

During the rest of the nineteenth century, many Americans would apply Beecher's tests: they would judge America in comparison with the past and by its liberation from what Beecher called "aristocratic tendencies," undemocracy in thought and institutions. Americans, in fact, would be more apt to feel they were *losing* democracy, not just failing to develop it. From these and other points of view there soon emerged plenty of opportunity for "melancholy prognostications" and the four fears.

Consider what was at hand:

• The rise of great industrial empires whose distant commands threatened the autonomy of local citizens: technology-based juggernauts, which seemed out of control in their very bent for control.

• The possibility that Americans would become either "tramps" or "millionaires," would divide into two great classes, eliminating the independent middle class; and that the upper class would further divide into rapacious magnates and a parasitical, effete 'second generation.'

• The sheer speedup of urbanization and industrial life, in contrast to the natural rhythms of rural folk, who were still a majority of the population and seemed to possess more authentic, organic communities.[22]

Behind all these visions there was the bewildering babel of immigration. As the 'new immigrants' from eastern and southern Europe started arriving in large numbers and packed into the tenements, older-stock Americans debated the nation's ability to absorb a mass of people who often seemed less prepared for democratic citizenship than for serving corrupt machines. As strikes and industrial violence fed middle-class fears of foreign agitators, the old, covert suspicion that democracy itself was a frail safeguard of order acquired a new force. "There is only one step beyond republicanism," proclaimed Illinois's state prosecutor at the Haymarket 'bomb-throwing' trial, "[and] that is anarchy."[23]

But champions of organized labor, too, could invoke the four fears. Adapting the language of the enlightened, self-made businessman that he was, John P. Altgeld spoke to all the fears in his inaugural address as governor of Illinois (1893).

> If we are to prosper we must make all of our people feel that the flag which flies over them is an emblem of justice. Our laboring people must either advance or retrograde. There is no such thing as standing still. If they are to advance it must be by their own conservative and intelligent standing together. Only those forces survive which can take care of themselves. The moment classes or individuals become dependent they are objects of charity, and their case is then hopeless. If the laboring classes cannot thus stand together, they will be reduced to the condition of the laboring classes in the old world.[24]

Altgeld's abhorrence of old-world class conditions was not new to his labor listeners. The fear of going the way of Europe's slums and 'serfs'—a fear that had colored the mutual stereotypes of North and South before the Civil War—was also a labor tradition. From the 1830s, as Herbert Gutman documented, there were immigrants and artisans who charged the factory system with betraying American promise and opportunity, and employed Revolutionary images in their attack on "money kings" and industrial "barons." They demonstrated that when workers were politicized, the fear of falling away was no more an upper-middle-class preserve than the fear of being owned.

The same concern about "degenerating into European conditions" and being *owned* by great combines, the same call to *restore* a Republic of the people, colored the rhetoric of the farmers' revolt. In looking back to Revolutionary symbols of freedom versus tyranny, yet forward to new economic policies and structures, the agrarian Populists met the double command of the fear of falling away: they would fulfill the past by constructing a new progress (even though they saw their legislative proposals as a way of checking decline and depredation rather than improving on the past).[25]

Urban middle-class reform, too, was quickened by the four fears. The concern with 'progress,' which meant finding the *right* progress; the fearful hope that America yet might redeem its failed promises; the wish to draw nation and community together in ways that would enhance rather than diminish the individual—impulses like these found a host of outlets in the proposals for renovating industrial society, from Henry George's widely read *Progress and Poverty* (1879) to the revival of Frederick Law Olmsted's ideas about the city park in the 1890s.* Olmsted believed that an urban "greensward" would produce fellowship as well as tranquillity among the park's users. It would reduce class differences and competitive stress and check the urban forces of "degeneration and demoralization." His doctrine acquired a new vogue at the end of the century, but the idea that the very pace and fragmentation of urban life was debilitating had been collecting supporters since the 1850s. The attention won by George Beard's book *American Nervousness* (1881) was merely a staging point in a long-growing suspicion that Americans were particularly prone to nervous exhaustion and related disorders.[26]

For some people, the solution to personal atrophy was not to eschew the city's stresses but to engage more fully with them. In her essay of 1892 on "The Subjective Necessity for Social Settlements," Jane Addams addressed the sensations of winding down and falling apart felt by herself and, so she said, other privileged young women of liberal background. When girls were raised on discussions of philanthropy and then warned against involvement with the poor; when they were "shut off" from the labor that served them and the "great starvation struggle" that was the most dynamic part of life, the result was a loss of personal unity between thought and action, a forlorn isolation from human fellowship, and a feeling of selfish and precarious advantage. Thus, for Addams, social separation meant personal disunion. Without its remedy—vigorous and constructive contact with other classes—the privileged young suffered, according to Addams, a shriveling of joy and sympathy and a loss of vitality.[27]

A more distinctly male response to urban life was to turn away from it, seeking in the wilderness or the West an antidote to overcivilized decadence. Among the eastern upper classes, the main movement for this began in the 1880s, but it was popularized and extended at the

---

*Concern about loss of community was not confined to radicals and reformers. Andrew Carnegie's famous essay on "Wealth" (*North American Review,* June 1889) starts with a nostalgic regard for a time of greater economic equality, when "the master and his apprentices" worked side by side. Carnegie justified modern inequality and social distance by arguing that specialization and big rewards for industrial leaders raised living standards generally. Nevertheless, his proposals for inducing those leaders to avoid personal ostentation and give much of their reward back to the whole society, to its institutions of culture and opportunity, reflected a wish to reintegrate as well as elevate the people.

turn of the century by figures like Ernest Thompson Seton, whose Woodcraft Indians pioneered the American scouting movement. Seton spoke almost simultaneously to the fears of winding down, being owned, and falling apart. The great foe was "degeneracy": "a large proportion of [America's] robust, manly, self-reliant boyhood" had turned into "a lot of flat-chested cigarette smokers with shaky nerves and doubtful vitality." The hordes of unemployed, whose ancient predecessors had helped cause the "decay" of Rome, had "never been taught to look after themselves" and so had become the "slaves" of professional agitators. Lest Americans follow the British into national decline, they should be alert to the fact that "every great nation" tended to become idle and slothful after "climbing laboriously to the zenith of its power."

Like George Beard, however, Seton also thought that an "over-busy life," along with too much specialization, depleted and reduced the individual. He disliked athletic competition, which, he believed, divided society between a mass of idle spectators and a "few overworked champions." His social ideal was a mystic campfire community where boys of different backgrounds lived together in "primitive brotherhood," pitting themselves not against each other but against universal standards of excellence and the "forces of Nature."[28]

Seton, unlike Theodore Roosevelt, was no militarist, but he shared with the hero of San Juan Hill a distrust of commercialism. Like other strenuous patriots of the time, both men wanted to save the nation from disintegrating into powerful but petty selfishness.[29] Some of these concerns were not unique to America. Imperialist anxieties about 'slackness' and lack of 'public spirit' were well known in Britain; commercialism and welfarism were both watched as potentially subversive. In different parts of Europe, too, racial and neo-Darwinist theories had joined with vaguer notions of *fin de siècle* decline to make 'degeneration' a commanding and versatile concept on both sides of the Atlantic.* Among other things, it entered the language of

---

*The concept found its Christopher Lasch in the Hungarian writer Max Nordau. Nordau's two-volume *Degeneration* (1892–93; English transl., 1895) used a medical and psychological vocabulary to describe a showy, false-visioned "ego-mania," a feverish yet ultimately passive fear of catastrophe, and several other tendencies identified by Lasch eight decades later. Nordau thought *fin de siècle* a silly term but found significance in its currency. His book received much attention, pro and con, in the American press. See also Brooks Adams, *The Law of Civilization and Decay: An Essay on History* (New York, 1898).

debate about the wisdom of extending women's roles. Feminists and antifeminists alike claimed their prescriptions would strengthen 'the race,' whereas their opponents were weakening it.[30]

But it was the frontier more than anything that put a distinctive stamp on American concerns with decline and decadence. The official 'closing' of the frontier, which Frederick Jackson Turner made so much of—the announcement of the 1890 U.S. Census that the West no longer contained an unbroken line of new settlement—only crystallized a belief that America's special source of dynamism and opportunity was near its end, that land was running out and too many immigrants were coming in. Although American life became more exuberant after the bad depression of the early nineties, popular books at the turn of the century began to celebrate the white Anglo-Saxon cowboy as a noble but dying breed, while politicians insisted hopefully that America would find new frontiers in expansionism abroad or nation-building at home.[31]

The beliefs that came out of all this were a curious mixture: often they stressed the importance of racial genes while being sensitive to the effects of geographic environment. In some popular fiction of the time, especially the writing of Frank Norris and Jack London, they produced an 'up or down' obsession. Plunged into a new terrain or situation, the heroes and heroines revert to a primitive self; genes or 'race memories' take over; and they either triumph or go under, sometimes sliding into horrible degradation. Such swings of personal fate were also allegories of American economics, the seesaw between boom and bust that shook so many lives.[32]

> For I knew, as I knew that I lived, that this ended the republic, as we had known it; that henceforward we Americans were to be part and parcel of world politics, rivalries, jealousies and militarism; that hate, prejudice and passion were now enthroned in the United States.

Oswald Garrison Villard, the New York liberal editor, wrote these words on the United States involvement in World War I long after it ended; but his feeling about Europe and America was commonplace in the American press in 1914–15 and was shared by Woodrow Wilson himself. Some of it was cockeyed—as if America had never grown its own "hate, prejudice and passion." Yet this showed how much Villard drew on a Revolutionary picture of republican purity and old-world depravity. Under the threat of European "militarism," the four fears could adopt a classical republican form. Villard's statement might almost have been lifted from George Washington's famous Farewell Address warning that entanglements abroad would drag the country down into foreign factionalism, self-betrayal, and the tyranny of passions (like Villard's "passion . . . *enthroned*").[33]

Yet Americans knew that foreign influence, in the shape of immigration, had already made them vulnerable to 'falling apart.' On the eve of war, about a third of the population was either foreign-born or had foreign-born parents, and many of these, due to their country of origin, felt no regard for the Allies. When the war (and wartime inflation) finally came to Americans, it remained unpopular with large sections of the working class, despite the patriotic fervor whipped up by the government and middle-class vigilante groups. However, in the wave of strikes that followed the end of the war and sparked off the 'red scare,' the forces of law and order usually managed to identify labor protest with alien and Bolshevik agitation.[34]

One effect of the 1917 Russian Revolution and the Sacco and Vanzetti case of 1921 was to fix again the tag 'undesirable alien' on central and southern Europeans (Germans were 'Nordic'). Against this background, and the wartime speedup in black migration to the North, old fears of racial degeneracy found new life. Writers like Madison Grant and Lothrop Stoddard anxiously affirmed that white Nordic civilization could stay vigorous and scale new heights, but only if it abandoned intermarriage, open immigration, and welfare policies that favored the 'lower races.'[35]

These attitudes found their most dramatic expression in the rise of the new Ku Klux Klan to political power, in the North as well as the South, through the early 1920s. (Its decline after 1925 was probably due to scandals of sex and violence, its extremist image and intensity, and the National Origins Act of 1924, whose immigrant quotas discriminated against non-WASPs and so preempted a Klan purpose.) Amid the dizzy cultural pluralism of the twenties, the Klan offered two kinds of union to hold on to: an abstract national patriotism based on the idea of white Protestant supremacy, and—like so many other secret fraternal orders in American history—a vivid local chapter of the like-minded, ritually sworn to fellowship and common service.

Against the fear of being owned by large and impersonal forces, the Klan established its own form of control. Within its clear-cut hierarchy it offered status and the chance of entrepreneurship. Kleagles (salesmen), King Kleagles (sales managers), and Grand Goblins (district sales managers) all received commissions on new memberships. The Klan did particularly well among Protestant newcomers in the fastest-growing cities, where it was easy for them to feel swept by. Psychologically, the Klan dealt with its foes and specters by mounting a solemn parody of them. Its rituals and hierarchy matched those of Catholicism, its fancy titles (Knight, King, Emperor, etc.) were un-American, and its in-group secrecy offset the larger invisibility of modern power.[36]

In their view of social developments, the Klan's exponents and defenders brought all four fears together; they articulated, in extreme form, anxieties shared by many Protestant traditionalists who never put on a white hood. Since the nineteenth century, as the Klan saw it, the forces of "mongrelization" had been stealing into America's spirit and taking it over (the fear of being owned). They had subverted and sullied its Christian principles and promise (the fear of falling away); they had divided and devitalized the people (the fears of falling apart and winding down). When religious traditions were ridiculed and the people demoralized, small wonder their birthrate was falling. Energies of the war had been sidetracked into crime, and "alien blocs" formed alliances against the public interest. Behind these blocs the directorate of Rome was working to snuff out American democracy and individualism. "Denatured intellectuals" could not understand this, but the common people (alerted by the Klan) were waking up to defend the purity of Nordic Americans and realize their "racial and national destiny" by returning to their pioneer strengths.[37]

Race and alienness were not the only sources of fear in the post–World War I period. As prosperity trickled down to the masses and installment buying became a popular institution, middle-class moralists and economic writers warned that hedonism was dethroning thrift and consumer self-indulgence undoing the worker's productivity. The Prohibition movement, indeed, had drawn on these anxieties as well as the idea of insidious control by the 'liquor interests.' The

Klan itself attacked impartially the bootlegger and the licentious spectacle of young male workers riding and reveling with their girlfriends in automobiles. In such pictures of bacchanalian decadence, the fears of winding down and falling apart came together.[38]

Even advertising, that engine of naughty extravagance, played on these anxieties. A number of ads suggested that modern civilization softened people with artificial luxuries while exhausting them with too much frantic bustle—the advertised product, however, would keep them crisp. In more subtle ways, advertisers' use of modern art designs often gave a sense of fragmentation, of jumbled breakup, leaving it to the copy and the product to provide resolution. Although advertising picked on these themes as a counterpoint to boom-time optimism, they were continued well past the '29 Crash into the early thirties.[39]

The relationship between the Great Depression and the four fears is curiously difficult to disentangle. The same is true for World War II. In both cases, the realities of an acute and prolonged emergency caused so much to be anxious about that it is often hard to pick out the traditional overtones of a fear. (I shall say little about World War II for just this reason.)

Despite the upheavals of the thirties, the fear of falling apart was less characteristic of that age—at least on a public level—than were the other fears. Yes, there were worries about revolt on the right and the left, about anger among the dispossessed; and as John Steinbeck so vividly described, California farmers and sheriffs excelled themselves in their paranoia toward the homeless, job-seeking 'Okies' as they poured in from the dust bowl. By and large, however, the Depression affected so many classes and sections that, in a sense, it brought people together—an effect represented in national politics by the 'Roosevelt coalition,' combining traditionally Republican groups with Democrats. If the shame of unemployment caused some to retreat into a shell, it also threw people together in welfare demands and vigilante action to prevent foreclosures. And because so much more of the population was rural than it is today, most families in poverty stayed intact. When the Okies drove out of the dust bowl, they mainly did so in family groups.[40]

The most striking expression of the other fears occurred in economics and in political rhetoric: in the 'Hansen theory' of stagnation (mainly a fear of winding down) and in the battle between Roosevelt and conservatives over the fear of being owned. Alvin Hansen's belief that rich, mature economies had a tendency to stagnate at high levels of unemployment acquired a substantial following among economists and public officials, not just in the thirties but in World War II, when many of them envisaged a postwar slump. Hansen was the leading American disciple of John Maynard Keynes, but he was also influenced by Turner. With the closing of the frontier and the end of rapid population growth, so Hansen believed, rigid and bureaucratic corporations could monopolize the economy, and they did so in a way that stunted real growth and investment. Hansen thus imputed to big business a deadening control (evoking the fear of being owned) which Americans had traditionally attributed to big government. Indeed, for Hansen and his followers, bigger government in the form of sustained federal investment and regulation of business were the saving remedies.[41]

Franklin Roosevelt was more explicit about switching targets. Defending the New Deal in 1936–37 against a variety of threats and rival schemes, he declared that "economic royalists" were the new equivalent of the "political autocracy" that the American people had fought in the Revolution. Through "democratic government," the Republic must restore itself and win freedom from "the privileged princes . . . of these new economic dynasties." Theirs was a monopoly power, which crushed "private enterprise" and "individual initiative" and "reached out for control over Government itself." In making these Jacksonian utterances on the issue of control and ownership, Roosevelt called the people back to "old truths" about democracy, virtue, and freedom. But his speech was also a summons to the future, against the fear of winding down and falling away.

> Shall we pause and turn our back upon the road that lies ahead? Shall we call *this* the promised land? Or, shall we continue on our way? For "each age is a dream that is dying, or one that is coming to birth."[42]

Roosevelt knew what he was up against in his efforts to legitimize expanded government. In 1935, when a fifth of the work force was officially estimated to be unemployed, a Gallup survey found that most adult Americans believed the federal government to be spending too much on relief and recovery, though most of them also supported various welfare measures and believed the government should take responsibility for full employment. Campaigning in 1936, the Republican vice-presidential candidate, Frank Knox, would have none of such ambivalence, at least not in public. "I preach to you," he cried, "the doctrine, not of the soft and kept spineless citizens of a regimented state, but of the self-respecting and self-reliant men who made America." His rhetoric made little headway in the election, but the studied fear of a Roosevelt federal dictatorship survived in enough corners of conservativism in the late thirties and wartime forties to help check liberal plans for a social-democratic reconstruction after the war.[43]

According to popular hindsight, the period extending from the Truman years through the election of Kennedy was a plateau of American confidence. U.S. industry had no rival in the world, and it seemed to be delivering the goods. In academe and press alike, influential commentators declared the United States to be an affluent, middle-class society where class differences were fading. The editors of *Fortune,* in a special issue on "U.S.A.—the Permanent Revolution" (February 1951), reported that American capitalism, in partnership with the political system, was uniquely fulfilling the nation's founding ideas. Material progress and spiritual values fed each other; labor unions had become agreeably bourgeois, while business leaders were at once enterprising individualists and community-minded civic organizers. Their main fault was that they didn't communicate abroad their nonmaterialist qualities. As the 1950s wore on, Americans were reminded that southern blacks and other undergroups did not share in the good news, but this was seldom seen as part of a general failure or falling apart of the system.

Much of the postwar climate, then, allayed the four fears. Yet there was another side to it, at least for the more educated. The alarm sounded by *The Organization Man* in 1956 was not just about conforming but about personal passivity and institutional decline. William Whyte's characters might work hard to climb the corporate ladder, but basically they were offering themselves up to an ossified institution in return for security and family comforts.

The fear that the country as a whole was winding down into fat and lethargy was addressed by John F. Kennedy's campaign theme: "I want this country to start moving again." The flabbiness could be spiritual too. In the early 1950s and again in the late 1950s–early '60s, there were waves of worry in the press and elsewhere about the moral state of the nation, as revealed by a variety of scandals. Among liberals there had also emerged by the late fifties a sense that the public domain was not holding the nation together. Philip Jacob's campus report of 1957, finding most college students to be "privatist" rather than public-spirited, was followed the next year by John Kenneth Galbraith's book *The Affluent Society,* which inspired the famous phrase "private affluence and public squalor," on run-down public services in a prosperous land. Both spoke to an incipient sense of falling apart.[44]

The Cold War sharpened all these anxieties; indeed, magazine articles about "apathy" and "moral breakdown" often related them to a total contest between two ways of life: Russia versus America, communism versus the West. Believing the Soviets to be rigorously trained spartans, patriotic critics attacked "permissiveness" and sloppy science teaching in the schools. Public policy officials, for their part, relayed a strenuous apprehension to each other as they strove to gird the nation's leadership for the international struggle of containing communism. In that struggle, as they saw it, every skill, every strength, every weakness would count; it was a test of "will" (favorite word of Cold War leaders), a summons to Americans to pull themselves together and project their historic values. Sometimes, indeed, exponents of "containment" became Puritan warriors, welcoming "the Communist threat" as a catalyst of effort and purpose. At the same time, ends and means were reversed. Statements of prized American values and goals became a tool, a spur to unity, dynamism, and international success.

It is against this background that one must understand Eisenhower's Commission on National Goals and other committee attempts to codify the nation's values and basic aims. In a long-term sense they simply reenacted the assumption that America was Americanism, a set of beliefs given form by the Founders and affirmed by immigrants and anti-immigrants alike. But why, then, the need to codify, and at this particular time? The answer, in part, is that leading Americans were *not* sure that their fellows shared *enough* of a sense of national purpose. The Korean War POW scandal, when large numbers of American prisoners were reported to have lost morale and collaborated with the enemy, seemed to show that Americans had not been taught a deep commitment to their

beliefs. Nor was it plain that the values they did share led necessarily to international endeavor. Isolationism had as good, or better,
an American pedigree.[45]

In dealing with isolationism, frontier images provided a handy
rhetoric. By linking old values and strengths to new futures, they also
addressed the fears of winding down and falling away. In this spirit,
NSC 68, the definitive National Security Council planning paper of
1950, gave a puritanical choice between constant struggle forward
and utter doom:

> For a free society there is never total victory, since freedom and
> democracy are never wholly attained, are always in the process of
> being attained. But defeat at the hands of the totalitarian is total
> defeat.

The notion of a permanent 'American Revolution' (matching the
communist one) merges here with the moving frontier.

In a more liberal quarter of the establishment, the term "new
frontier" was used by Chester Bowles in 1953, long before it become
the Kennedy administration's nickname. Writing about his ambassa-
dorship to India, Bowles called on Americans to "rediscover" their
pioneer virtues by joining in "this country's main adventure," assist-
ing and working with different peoples in "every undeveloped continent and country." Much of what Bowles said foreshadowed *The Ugly
American* (1958), that best-seller of counterinsurgency, whose heroes
become real frontiersmen. They go into "the sticks" to live among
Asian villagers, providing them with the aid they really need (it would
later be called 'intermediate technology') while giving no time to the
"princes of bureaucracy."[46]

What, though, of the fear of being owned? It appeared most obviously in McCarthyite specters of communist infiltration and takeover.
It also showed up, as I said earlier, in the claim by Riesman, Whyte,
and others that organizations and indeed society itself owned too
much of the individual's emotional life. Toward the end of the 1950s,
some of the fear of being owned was pinpointed on media manipulators, "hidden persuaders." But the fear's most striking new feature
was the belief that people were likely to surrender themselves to a
general group conformism. Although the media might help induce
this, the causes were generally considered more diffuse. Suspicion
that Americans might be especially prone to conformity was not

new—it went back through Sinclair Lewis and H. L. Mencken in the twenties to Tocqueville and other foreign commentators in the early nineteenth century—but it did not become a widespread, upper-middle-class concern until after World War II.[47]

The more complex thought that what produced conformity might also, on a deeper plane, drive people apart did not receive much attention in the 1950s. A few voices on the left did complain that the go-getting, status-seeking pace of suburban life gave little chance for people really to know each other; and as early as 1951, C. Wright Mills argued that pseudofriendly commercialism—the marketing of one's personality to manipulate others—had sown an "all-pervasive distrust" through the middle classes. In the main, though, spontaneity, not closeness, seemed the scarce good. It took the 1960s 'counterculture,' as I have already suggested, to bring the two lines of criticism firmly together: to claim that middle-class, suburban America suppressed true individualism while isolating people in synthetic and competitive relations. Many of the young Appalachian Volunteers of the 1960s, who went as poverty workers into Kentucky and West Virginia, voiced this critique of the America they had left behind. In the mountain communities of Appalachia they hoped to find (and did find) "a place within a place": an identity within a family network of close and genuine relationships.[48]

The Port Huron Statement, founding document of the 'new left,' was issued by SDS (Students for a Democratic Society) in 1962, and it summoned all four fears. The fear of being owned came easily enough, for SDS claimed that the modern state assaulted the individual's capacity for "self-direction" and produced instead a "manipulated acquiescence." More significant in a document of militant protest, which might be expected to have no fear of disruption, was the concern about falling apart. The concern was not just tactical, a matter of bridging the gulf between middle-class students and labor; it was also part of a political and social belief. "Participatory democracy" was SDS's alternative to a power system that fomented anarchy abroad and, at home, "estrangement between man and man."

The fear of winding down followed from this: the overwhelming forces that produced cynicism and apathy in individuals robbed the nation of "community, impulse, inner momentum." Hope, however, leavened the fear of falling away. Degraded work, bigotry, inequality, had betrayed American ideals, but new initiatives had appeared on the scene, among civil rights workers, in the peace movement, and in labor; they required, however, a "vision" of what was possible.

That vision, the SDS ideal of a fairer, more loving society in the control of its ordinary members, survived all the turmoil of the sixties, but it became angrier, more bloodshot, as the Vietnam War divided the nation. And against the background of assassinations, riots, and campus disruptions, the fear of falling apart had to feature prominently in the backlash against the new left. In his speech of 1968 accepting the Republican nomination for President, Richard Nixon offered balm for this fear, as he did for the fear of falling away. By healing and unifying the nation, restoring order at home and greatness abroad, he would lead the country back to its traditional path of economic and social progress, "the world's greatest continuing revolution, the American Revolution."[49]

Such progress was not to be. By the end of the 1960s, inflation had started to wipe out real pay increases, and unemployment had started its long trend upward. Between 1973 and 1984, median household income fell by 6 percent, and average individual earnings slumped 14 percent. Big money was made at the top and in finance, but many young professionals felt the squeeze. Although spending stayed high, more and more of it was financed by debt, indirectly by foreigners as the U.S. started importing more than it exported. In 1985, for the first time since 1919, foreigners owned more U.S. assets than Americans owned abroad.[50]

In the realm of the four fears, the most obvious effect was to inflame the fear of winding down. Most Americans, when surveyed, affirmed their belief in the basic U.S. system and its "special role" in the world, but trust in their leaders (government, business, union, and so on) declined sharply after Kennedy. According to various polls in the seventies and eighties, more and more Americans (though usually a minority) doubted that things would improve in the future—either for the nation in a general way or, economically, for themselves and their children.[51]

As the press picked up these reports, commentators amplified their effects by declaring that faith in progress and the American Dream was fading. A retired corporate president told Studs Terkel in 1978:

I think our nation has grown old, and very rapidly. We've lost a lot of the Dream. We're like people my age, whose world narrows. A young man comes out of school and he's interested in everything. Then he gets a job and his world narrows a bit. He marries. Job, home, family. And it narrows a bit more. Finally, he gets older. Through with his job, his family gone away, his ultimate concern is his bowel movement every morning. Our country is going through a great deal of that now.

Some of this was the personal projection of a lonely aging man's anxieties: he admitted to Terkel that business competitiveness had deprived him of close friends. But his statement was, even more than he intended, a parable of the nation. It expressed the "Me Decade's" conflict between two kinds of individualism: 'specialize and go for it' versus 'expand oneself and enjoy.' Both types of individualism, it suggested, could lead to a blinkered obsession with oneself—the visionless dead-end street pictured by Christopher Lasch. Nevertheless, it offered a glimmer of hope: the last sentence hinted that the nation might just be going through a phase.[52]

It is perhaps no coincidence that inner frontiersmanship—the quest for psychological experience—flourished in the decade of OPEC, the energy crisis, and worries about large-scale pollution, when outer frontiersmanship—faith in ceaseless economic expansion—was being challenged.[53] But inner migrations could not compensate everyone. In some quarters of opinion, the new sense of national limits did not just fan the fear of winding down; it also fitted a line of criticism that went beyond the fear of falling away by attacking the very sources of American promise. At a time of heavy U.S. bombing of Vietnam, the runaway sales of Dee Brown's *Bury My Heart at Wounded Knee* (1971) helped establish a new beachhead in American upper-middle-class consciousness: the realization that the frontier-expansionist tradition contained a history of genocide.[54] Through most of the seventies and early eighties—a period, ironically, when right-wing economists and 'neoconservative' intellectuals flourished—critics of market capitalism largely dominated the new interpretations of American social history.

Even the Founders did not escape. In 1972, America's most distinguished colonial historian, Edmund Morgan, said he had changed his mind on the relation between slavery and the origins of the Republic. Once, he had assumed that slavery was just a dreadful aberration of early American democracy. Now he believed that the two were deeply entwined, that the great Virginian statements of (white) freedom and equality were nurtured in complex ways by a slaveholding system.[55]

These revisions, however, did not command a wide enough support to remove the fear of falling away by eliminating its premise, the belief that America's founding traditions contained special virtues. Interpreters of American life and character were still more likely to perceive declension than original sin. For some of them, indeed, ecological limits to national growth could be used to restore old qualities of hardy thrift and practical inventiveness, and to rebuild communities where people had time for each other in a simpler, more natural way of life.[56]

These yearnings came together in Jimmy Carter's extraordinary television address of July 15, 1979. Originally planned as one of a series on energy policy, it was also concerned, as Carter said, with "deeper" problems of the national spirit. All four fears found a place in the speech. Carter had read and extolled Lasch's *Culture of Narcissism,* and Daniel Yankelovich was one of the throng of leading Americans whom he had self-consciously consulted before the speech. The President was also influenced by his own pollster, Pat Cadell, who three years before had pronounced America to be a "goal-oriented country which [had] lost its sense of goals."[57]

Part of the background to Carter's address was the oil shortage, causing angry scenes and even violence in lines of cars at the gas pumps. Most speeches by modern Presidents and presidential candidates avoid criticizing the people themselves for being led astray. Carter's was different. It was a mixture of confession and jeremiad. He blamed himself for lack of leadership; he blamed the people for abandoning their traditions. (He also said he had drawn on the grass-roots wisdom of ordinary folk, but that is a standard claim in American political rhetoric.)

Carter's speech reviewed a familiar list of affronts to American self-esteem. It included the Vietnam War, Watergate, and mounting pessimism itself, though it made no reference to Japan or the close-down of factories ('deindustrialization' was then a rising issue). In dealing with energy problems, Carter touched indirectly on the fear of being owned: the phrase "dependence on foreign oil" appeared three times, along with related words: "dependency," "independent." But his main theme was built on a unity among the three other fears: of falling apart, winding down, and falling away. Divided by special interests and a spirit of no compromise, Americans had lost that confidence in progress which, according to Carter, had founded the nation. Sacrificing the pride that once came from "hard work, strong families, close-knit communities and our faith in God," Americans now chose "self-indulgence and consumption."

In presenting specific measures for saving energy and developing alternatives to oil, Carter invested them with symbolic value. If Americans would "join hands" in support of it, the program could "rekindle our sense of unity, our confidence in the future, and give us a new sense of purpose."[58]

By and large, Americans were not impressed by the speech. Although many shared his moral views (they were not just those of a southern Baptist), people were unused to such plaintiveness from a President, and his energy program did not excite them. As the U.S. went into economic recession, the upbeat language of Ronald Reagan offered a more attractive solution to the nation's fears. He, too, spoke of restoring national pride and unity and family virtue, but he also rejected the concept of ecological limits to growth. A vigorous consumer market would, he believed, stimulate investment and open up new sources of energy.

In the fall of 1984, when most experts had declared the recession over, the editors of *Time* magazine put a leaping Uncle Sam on the cover and made "America's Buoyant Mood" their cover story. The article conceded, however, that much of the buoyancy might be a superficial fizz, even perhaps just a media hype. Only the future would tell if it became a selfish complacency. By mid-1987 (the time of this writing), a series of public scandals in finance, sex, and politics had persuaded *Time*'s editors that the nation's morale was again in danger. "Whatever happened to ETHICS," one of their covers declared, without a question mark. "Assaulted by sleaze, scandals and hypocrisy, America searches for its moral bearings."[59]

This, too, may have been a media exaggeration; but *Time* knows its market, and it probably picked up something in its readership. When the economy falters, articulate Americans fear that the country has lost its dynamism. And when the economy (or part of it) booms, especially under administrations that seek to liberate big business, the result seems to be a wave of high-placed corruption which generates a fear of moral decay. There is always cause for hope, and always something to worry about.*

*In the wake of 'Irangate' indictments and a hostile educated opinion, it is easy to forget the enormous fan mail received by Lieutenant Colonel Oliver North during his televised testimony before the Senate investigating committee in 1987. The 'Ollie' boom soon vanished (like General Douglas MacArthur's in 1951), and most Americans continued to oppose aid to the Nicaraguan 'contras,' and therefore opposed North's Central American activities. Nevertheless, he exhibited a mixture of innocence and ruthlessness, which many Americans admire. Just as Joe McCarthy drew popular support by standing up to the State Department and fighting the good but dirty fight against traitors—just as *Rambo* refought the Vietnam War as a lone, brave individual—so Ollie North, the marine, stood up to the senators, exposed their vacillations, and made it all simple. He was his own man, restoring to the people a sense of independence, vigor, and even (wonder of wonders) moral purpose.

Epilogue

I have shown in this book some ambivalence to the study of American character. Essentially I like the enterprise, which is obvious since I practice it myself. Americans have a refreshing readiness to put their feet on the desk and open up about themselves and others, to sit back from the hard data that pervades their lives, and speculate and generalize about shifting moods and motives. On an academic level, the same sensitivity to group attitudes and styles enriches the writing of American history.

But the business of interpreting American character can also be a snare, especially the market in lamentation that has flourished since the mid-sixties, in newspaper columns and literary essays as well as in systematic studies. It is not just that the lamentation is exaggerated and one-sided, as I argued in Chapter 3. The obsession with middle-class states of mind trivializes the more substantial costs paid by people who are mainly *not* middle class—costs ranging from job insecurity to malnutrition.[1]

The real problem of America, as I see it, is not that the system desolates most people. It provides many with a good quality of life, but that life is excessively protected by corporate and government power, which at home could do more to reduce poverty and abroad has permitted an array of covert operations—by private groups as well as the CIA—to foment violence against radical socialist movements and governments even when they are basically indigenous.

Of course, American social attitudes affect the power system. Elite attitudes help to shape it; popular attitudes cynically accept it.[2] But we do not need the psychological theories of a Jules Henry or a

113

Christopher Lasch to explain these attitudes. They rest on simpler traditions and beliefs.

For example, I accept the assertion that many Americans, including working-class people, endorse economic inequality to give their children (if not themselves) a chance of 'making it.' Surveys and interviews have revealed this attitude, though they have also shown that most Americans prefer a limited inequality, giving the poorest household about half the median income. I would not reject, either, the more speculative notion, implied by Michael Lewis in *The Culture of Inequality* (1978), that competitive society leaves far more people feeling failures than they let on. But when Lewis declares that Americans oppose poverty programs because it comforts them to have worse failures around, or when Philip Slater claims that Americans attack collectivist radicals because secretly they want to be collectivists too, then social-character theories become psychiatric smears.

What, then, of my own theory of American character, stressing the play of four fears in the nation's history and culture? In a few cases— secession and the Civil War, for instance, or the rise of the second Ku Klux Klan—the influence of the four fears has been decisive. In most of American history, however, the four fears have merely reinforced other factors. They have helped form the language in which social and political problems are addressed; they have supplied a set of symbols and emotions for lining up support behind a policy or candidate.

To me the four fears represent both good and bad. The fear of being owned has served many causes of freedom and equality, yet it has also been used to block government provision for the needy. The fear of falling apart has been used to promote community and civic action, yet it has also inflamed racist paranoia and the repression of radicals. The fear of winding down has partnered American dynamism and zest. It has also incited self-aggrandizement, a refusal to accept decent and necessary limits, and expansion for its own sake. The fear of falling away from a special American promise has powered idealism and reform in public life. It has also advanced the conceit that the United States has a duty to enlighten and purify the world.

The assumption that Americans are at source the most natural and decent people; that their kind of democracy and freedom is what people everywhere will naturally choose (as so many immigrants chose America)—all this supports the belief that America must fulfill itself by propagating 'progress' and 'democracy' everywhere. It blocks the thought that American policies could actually be seen by foreigners as a threat to their own freedoms.* These attitudes correspond to what scholars often call the 'universalistic' strain in American foreign policy. Theoretically, it contradicts a 'realpolitik' strain; in practice, the two complement each other. Realpolitik is more subject to the fear of winding down than to the fear of falling away. It takes a hard-nosed view of interests to be defended; it accepts right-wing dictatorships and juntas as allies, so long as they remain stable, since they are against communism and they generally permit U.S. corporations to flourish on their soil. The moralizing, 'universalistic' strain, which calls for liberal democracy, operates mainly against communist regimes or declining right-wing ones. The history of the U.S. and the Philippines under Marcos illustrates this perfectly: support for Marcos until his position was untenable, then support for Aquino's form of democracy.

These are hard words from someone who grew up as a small beneficiary of Marshall aid and, as an even smaller (and skinnier) inmate of a Japanese internment camp, may have owed his life to American dash and power—an advance force of GIs who penetrated Manila one night in 1944 and surprised our captors. Yet I believe that in U.S. foreign relations the fear of falling away and, even more, the fear of winding down have been made a danger to other peoples. They characterize in particular some of the most activist foreign-policy officials, who feel they must vanquish the isolationism that infects the benighted populace.

The most destructive effect of the fear of winding down is the tendency to label an adversary's slightest achievement as a foreign-policy reverse and to treat any communist or socialist revolution as a dire threat even when it is essentially home-grown (e.g., Guatemala in the fifties, Chile in the seventies). By exaggerating the hand of Soviet power or international communism in these events, the country's exponents of strenuous fear simultaneously neglect and subvert the domestic achievements of left-wing governments in reducing poverty, child mortality, and so on (as has happened in Cuba and Nicaragua). The prejudices of U.S. policymakers become self-confirming as they drive these governments into heavy military spending and greater dependence on Soviet rather than U.S. trade and finance.

*See Raymond Bonner, *Waltzing with a Dictator: The Marcoses and the Making of Foreign Policy* (New York, 1987); Bryan Johnson, *The Four Days of Courage: The Untold Story of the People Who Brought Marcos Down* (New York, 1987).

The tendency to see the world as one big contest, where you can only win or lose, is based on a psychological domino theory. According to this, the important thing is to *signal* strength, not weakness, to allies and enemies. During the Vietnam War, it was thought that if South Vietnam 'fell,' U.S. allies would fall away too, and communist rebels, taking heart, would spring up all over the place. It didn't happen, but the same kind of fear continues in a concept of psychological 'linkage,' the belief that what the U.S. does or does not do in one place will determine its standing in others. (It is a somber thought that Henry Kissinger, a leading exponent of this idea, flourishes today as a wise owl of foreign affairs. His responsibility for the massive, secret, and disastrous bombing of Cambodia, done largely to project strength to the North Vietnamese following their limited occupation of Cambodian 'sanctuaries,' has not dented his career as a consultant and speaker.[3])

Admittedly, the assumptions underlying psychological linkage are not just American. They draw from memories of the Munich Conference, 1938, when signals of British and French weakness did encourage Hitler (though at that belated point they won time for British rearmament). The concept also reflects big-power tensions in a nuclear age: the less you can use your ultimate weapons, the more you plot your moves in terms of psychological deterrence, 'credibility,' and so forth. But historic American self-consciousness, going back to John Winthrop's sermon ("the eyes of all people are upon us"), has given this outlook a fertile ground.

> In Central America, too, the cause of freedom is being tested. And our resolve is being tested there as well. Here, especially, the world is watching to see how this nation responds.

These words of Ronald Reagan, defending U.S. support for Nicaragua's 'contras,' were part of a tradition that found new life in the Cold War—numerous statements by U.S. leaders have said essentially the same thing.[4]

America's physical isolation, cushioning it from foreign wars, has had two opposite effects on the fear of winding down. For many people, especially the less educated, who do not think internationally, it alleviates fear: they just don't believe that what happens in Nicaragua can send America 'down the tubes.' Sometimes, however, the lack of any experience at living close to foreign wars and political instability causes a panic exaggeration of danger from abroad—hence the mass cancellation of plane bookings to Europe after the bombing of Libya. I think this also helps explain the treatment of Japanese-Americans in World War II, not just their wholesale imprisonment but their harassment by local citizens before and after.[5] The belief, too, that the U.S. is a created *idea,* a set of principles of freedom and democracy, can make it seem all the more vulnerable to foreign subversion: ideas don't have to swim the Rio Grande.

At the same time, ironically, U.S. dependence on a global network of alliances, with their corresponding hostilities, creates more points at which the 'national interest' can receive a setback, more opportunities for the fears of winding down and falling apart. In a subtle way it may also sharpen the sense of being owned, as George Washington warned in his Farewell Address of 1796:

> The nation which indulges toward another an habitual hatred or an habitual fondness is in some degree a slave. It is a slave to its animosity or to its affection, either of which is sufficient to lead it astray from its duty and its interest. Antipathy in one nation against another disposes each more readily to offer insult and injury, to lay hold of slight causes of umbrage, and to be haughty and intractable when accidental or trifling occasions of dispute occur.[6]

The path of wisdom lies not in rejecting the four fears altogether— they are too entrenched in American history and character for that— but in channeling them into constructive action and refusing to yield the high ground of patriotism and strength to those who practice callous policies from luxury bunkers. Going back to John Peter Altgeld and long before, many politicians have shown it can be done, but the task needs a more sustained effort.

Like other facets of social character, the four fears are not a precise ideology. If they exclude complete socialism at home, they are compatible with many options short of this. As I have already suggested, the most important political aspect of the four fears is that they affect the language and symbols in which policies are considered. Americans who wish to renovate their system, and foreigners who need to negotiate with Americans, will do well to touch base with this language.

Notes

1. An Industry

1. Christopher Lasch, *The Culture of Narcissism: American Life in an Age of Diminishing Expectations* (New York, 1979); Lasch, *The Minimal Self: Psychic Survival in Troubled Times* (New York, 1984). Cf. Lasch, *Haven in a Heartless World: The Family Besieged* (New York, 1977). Lasch's belief that he was explaining more than America emerged at a British conference where another panelist disagreed: see discussion between Lasch and Michael Rustin in Barry Richards, ed., *Capitalism and Infancy: Essays on Psychoanalysis and Politics*, "Family and Authority" (Atlantic Highlands, N.J., and London, 1984). The attention to current and recent social character is one of the things that distinguish Lasch and his American predecessors from the *mentalité* school of European historians.

2. James Baldwin, "The Discovery of What It Means to Be an American," *New York Times Book Review* (January 25, 1959), reprinted in Baldwin, *Nobody Knows My Name: More Notes of a Native Son* (New York, 1961), pp. 3–12; cf. pp. 20–22, 83.

On other concepts of social character and culture, cf. George De Vos, "National Character," *International Encyclopaedia of the Social Sciences* (New York, 1968), vol. XI, pp. 14–19.

3. F. J. Turner's paper, given at the American Historical Association's 1893 meeting, was reprinted in his book *The Frontier in American History* (New York, 1920).

4. Cf. Barbara Ehrenreich, *The Hearts of Men: American Dreams and the Flight from Commitment* (New York, 1983); *U.S. News & World Report* (June 3, 1985), series on "The American Male" (including "Beyond Macho—the Search for Self" and "Women: The View from the Majority"). However, generalizations about national moods and group attitudes in magazines and newspapers are less distinctively American than in books: they occur, for example, in France and Germany.

5. Examples are detailed in Rupert Wilkinson, "American Character Revisited," *Journal of American Studies* 17 (1983), pp. 167–68. More recently, even George C. Lodge, *The American Disease* (New York, 1984), which focused mainly on economic and business policies, declared that America's economic "disease [was] importantly a psychological ailment": p. 15.

6. This literature and rhetoric is discussed in the sequel to this book: Rupert Wilkinson, ed., *American Social Character: Modern Interpretations* (in the British comparative section of the bibliographical essay). Recently, in a wave of enthusiasm about Britain's economic resurgence and world "standing," Margaret Thatcher expressed a more favorable view of British social character: "It is in the British character to take responsibility, to show . . . enterprise." BBC interview by David Dimbleby (January 25, 1988).

7. Discussed, ibid. On post–Boer War anxieties about British character, see also Jefferson Hunter, *Edwardian Fiction* (Cambridge, Mass., 1982). Cf. C. F. G. Masterman, *The Condition of England* (London, 1909). "England Your England" was Part I of George Orwell's pamphlet *The Lion and the Unicorn* (London, 1941) and is reprinted in his *Collected Essays, Journalism and Letters,* ed. by Sonia Orwell and Ian Angus (Harmondsworth, 1965), vol. II, pp. 74–79; cf. Orwell, "The English People." *Evening Standard* (London, December 15, 1945), reprinted in Orwell's *Collected Essays . . .* (Harmondsworth, 1968), vol. III, pp. 15–56. See Geoffrey Gorer, *Exploring English Character* (London, 1955); cf. Gorer, "English Character in the Twentieth Century," *Annals of the American Academy of Political and Social Science* 44 (March 1967), pp. 74ff. Since Gorer, the only full-scale study of modern British social-character trends is Daniel Snowman's Anglo-American comparison, *Britain and America: An Interpretation of British and American Culture 1945–1975* (New York, 1977; British title, *Kissing Cousins*).

8. Herbert G. Eldridge, "The Paper War Between England and America: The *Inchiquin* Episode," *Journal of American Studies* 16 (1982), pp. 49–68.

9. I am grateful to Robert A. Gross for the essential idea of these three phases, although I have revised the third one. The phrase, "special commission," is from John Winthrop's sermon of 1630, "A Modell of Christian Charity."

10. Cf. Marie Jahoda, "The Migration of Psychoanalysis: Its Impact on American Psychology," *Perspectives in American History* 2 (1968), pp. 420–25.

11. David M. Potter, "The Quest for the National Character," in John Higham, ed., *The Reconstruction of American History* (New York, 1962). More relevant, perhaps, is Higham's own observation that America's ethnic mix contains a larger number of groups, relatively equal in size, than that of most other immigrant nations, which tend to "draw disproportionately from a few favored ethnic backgrounds": Higham, *Send These to Me: Jews and Other Immigrants in Urban America* (New York, 1975), pp. 14–18. It is easier to encourage, or at least envisage, a melting pot of national character drawn from many "small" ethnic contributions (albeit dominated by northern European Protestants) than a character that has to cut across one or two major ethnic divisions. In "The Dispraising of America" (based on a 1959 talk), John

A. Kouwenhoven attributed the appetite of Americans for identifying and criticizing their social character to the "double citizenship" of an immigrant people whose Revolution had *voluntarily* and uniquely (for a "major world power") shattered their old world ties. But didn't the Mexican rebellions and other Latin American revolts do the same? Kouwenhoven's explanation is insufficient, but added to Higham's point above it may be valid. See Kouwenhoven, *The Beer Can by the Highway: Essays on What's 'American' about America* (New York, 1961).

12. David Riesman et al., *The Lonely Crowd: A Study of the Changing American Character* (New Haven, 1950), ch. 9, sec. 3 ("The Inside Dopesters").

13. For other views of the history and social background of writing on American character, see Thomas L. Hartshorne, *The Distorted Image: Changing Conceptions of the American Character Since Turner* (Cleveland, 1968), which takes the story up to the 1950s but excludes foreign writers; David M. Potter, *People of Plenty: Economic Abundance and the American Character* (Chicago, 1954), part I; Alex Inkeles and Daniel J. Levinson, "National Character," in Gardner Lindzey and Elliott Aronson, eds., *Handbook of Social Psychology* (2nd ed., 1968), vol. IV, pp. 418–23; Luther S. Luedke, "The Search for American Character," in Luedke, ed., *Making America: The Society and Culture of the United States* (Washington, D.C., 1987), which is best on the 1930s and '40s; Richard H. Pells, *The Liberal Mind in a Conservative Age: American Intellectuals in the 1940s and '50s* (New York, 1985); Jesse F. Battan, "The 'New Narcissism' in 20th-Century America: The Shadow and Substance of Social Change," *Journal of Social History* 17 (1983), pp. 199–220. My article (Wilkinson, note 5 above) among other things classifies modern theories of American character according to type of explanation: economic versus cultural; "continuity versus change"; and American "exceptionalism" versus international trends. Perhaps the best historical background to social character writing of the 1940s–80s is William F. Chafe, *The Unfinished Journey: America Since World War II* (New York, 1986), esp. ch. 5, 14, 15.

2. A Literature

General note. A fuller bibliography of writing on American character 1940s–80s, is given in the sequel to this book, *American Social Character: Modern Interpretations,* ed. Rupert Wilkinson.

1. Margaret Mead, *And Keep Your Powder Dry: An Anthropologist Looks at America* (New York, 1942; British title, *The American Character*). Cf. Mead, "Why We Americans Talk Big," BBC broadcast printed in *The Listener* (London, October 28, 1943).

2. Geoffrey Gorer, *The American People: A Study in National Character*

(New York, 1948). The psycho-anthropological tradition developed by Mead also produced Erik H. Erikson's dense and difficult "Reflections on the American Identity," which related a complex but fundamentally rejecting "Mom" figure to several historical factors, and to standardization, pseudo-individualism, and a basic polarity between sitting still and moving out. Erikson, *Childhood and Society* (New York, 1950), ch. 8.

3. Harold J. Laski, *The American Democracy* (London, 1949). My exegesis does not reveal Laski's contradictory positions on the importance of the frontier—discussed in my sequel to this volume, *American Social Character: Modern Interpretations,* in the bibliographical essay. Laski's relatively benign view of American character, despite his socialism, expressed a lifelong commitment to freedom and pluralism; it may also have reflected the interest of some prewar Labor Party politicians in the experimentalism of the New Deal. Cf. Kenneth O. Morgan, *Labour People: Leaders and Lieutenants, Hardie to Kinnock* (London, 1987), pp. 93ff.

4. Ralph Barton Perry, *Characteristically American* (New York, 1949), esp. ch. 1 ("The American Cast of Mind").

5. David Riesman, with Nathan Glazer and Reuel Denney, *The Lonely Crowd: A Study of the Changing American Character* (New Haven, 1950). It was followed by a volume of case studies: David Riesman, with Nathan Glazer, *Faces in the Crowd: Individual Studies in Character and Politics* (New Haven, 1951). The introduction to this sequel abandons *The Lonely Crowd's* notion of a link between social-character types and stages of population growth. My summary makes little of it too. Riesman had second thoughts on the issue in his 1961 preface to *The Lonely Crowd,* pp. xlii–xliv in the 1969 Yale paperback.

6. On loneliness, see Riesman et al. (note 5 above), pp. v–vi, 168, 170, 372–73 in the original 1950 edition; also pp. 69–70, 155 in the slightly abridged 1969 Yale paperback. The latter omits "lonely member of the crowd" etc. (pp. v–vi in the original edition).

7. William H. Whyte, Jr., *The Organization Man* (New York, 1956).

8. David M. Potter, "The Quest for the National Character," in John Higham, ed., *The Reconstruction of American History* (New York, 1962); Potter, "American Individualism in the Twentieth Century," *Texas Quarterly* (Summer 1963), revised and reprinted in Gordon Mills, ed., *Innocence and Power: Individualism in Twentieth-Century America* (Austin, 1965); Potter, "American Women and American Character," *Stetson University Bulletin* 62 (January 1962), pp. 1–22, reprinted in Michael McGiffert, ed., *The Character of Americans: A Book of Readings* (Homewood, Ill., 1964; rev. ed., 1970).

9. Quoted by David M. Potter, *People of Plenty: Economic Abundance and the American Character* (Chicago, 1954), pp. 153–54. Cf. F. J. Turner, "The

Significance of the Frontier in American History" (1893), reprinted in Turner, *The Frontier in American History* (New York, 1920).

10. "A Changing American Character?" is ch. 3 of Seymour Martin Lipset, *The First New Nation: The United States in Historical and Comparative Perspective* (New York, 1963). An earlier version of this essay appeared in Lipset and Leo Lowenthal, eds., *Culture and Social Character: The Work of David Riesman Reviewed* (New York, 1961). Lipset's speculation about convention and "psychic energy" was quoted from Clyde Kluckholn, "Have There Been Discernible Shifts in American Values During the Past Generation?" in Elting E. Morison, ed., *The American Style: Essays in Value and Performance* (New York, 1958), p. 187.

11. A precursor of this trend was C. Wright Mills, *White Collar* (New York, 1951), which departed from Riesman et al. in claiming that marketing-oriented personalities sowed distrust. See p. 107.

12. George W. Pierson, "The Moving American," *Yale Review* 44 (Autumn 1954), pp. 99–111; Pierson, "The M-Factor in American History," *American Quarterly* 14 (Summer 1962 Supplement), pp. 275–89; Pierson, "Under a Wandering Star," *Virginia Quarterly Review* 39 (Autumn 1963), pp. 621–38; Pierson, "A Restless Temper . . . ," *American Historical Review* 69 (July 1964), pp. 969–89. Pierson's "restless temper" quotation is from Tocqueville's diary for June 7, 1831: Alexis de Tocqueville, *Journey to America,* ed. J. P. Mayer, transl. George Laurence (New Haven, 1960), pp. 182–83. Pierson discussed the institutional and economic effects of mobility as well as the character effects. He subsequently collected and elaborated his articles in a book, *The Moving American* (New York, 1973).

13. The last quotation is from Pierson's 1964 article (note 12 above).

14. Jules Henry, *Culture Against Man* (New York, 1963). Henry said he "started to write, or rather, to rewrite" the book in 1956, and then revised it again after 1958.

15. Charles Reich, *The Greening of America* (New York, 1970).

16. Philip E. Slater, *The Pursuit of Loneliness: American Culture at the Breaking Point* (Boston, 1970; rev. ed., 1976). My summary is based on the 1970 edition. Cf. Slater, *Wealth Addiction* (New York, 1980).

17. Michael Kammen, *People of Paradox: An Inquiry Concerning the Origins of American Civilization* (New York, 1972), is really about American character, past and present, but it focuses on American dualism per se rather than on the substance of attitudes and values. On this and other social-character writing in the 1960s and '70s, see Rupert Wilkinson, "American Character Revisited," *Journal of American Studies* 17 (1983), pp. 171–76. As the word *mentalité* suggests, the question of changing social character and attitudes interested 'early modern' historians of France and Europe; but their interest did not lead to much writing on more recent trends.

18. Michael Lewis, *The Culture of Inequality* (Amherst, 1978).

19. On the "Me Decade," see Tom Wolfe's collection of essays *Mauve Gloves and Madmen, Clutter and Vine* (New York, 1976). For longer-term transnational and comparative views of the 'sensate culture,' see Daniel Bell, *The Cultural Contradictions of Capitalism* (New York, 1976; summarized in a new, long foreword, 1979 ed.); Daniel Snowman, *Britain and America: An Interpretation of British and American Culture, 1945–1975* (New York, 1977; British title, *Kissing Cousins*).

20. Christopher Lasch, *The Culture of Narcissism: American Life in an Age of Diminishing Expectations* (New York, 1979); cf. Lasch, *The Minimum Self: Psychic Survival in Troubled Times* (New York, 1984); also comments on Lasch, Charles Reich, and American culture in Paul Wachtel, *The Poverty of Affluence: A Psychological Portrait of the American Way of Life* (New York, 1983).

21. David Riesman, "Egocentrism: Is the American Character Changing?" *Encounter* 55 (August–September 1980), pp. 19–28.

22. Daniel Yankelovich, *New Rules: Searching for Self-Fulfillment in a World Turned Upside Down* (New York, 1981), was preceded by a long article excerpting much of the book's text: Yankelovich, "New Rules in American Life," *Psychology Today* (April 1981), pp. 35ff. Yankelovich said he was writing not about "social character" (which he associated with surviving traditional values) but about a faster-changing "psycho-culture." He defined this, however, as the "meanings," "inner processes," and "consciousness" Americans had in common—not a bad definition of social character! And in spite of rejecting Lasch's observations of narcissism, he himself espied "narcissistic tendencies" in the seventies. Yankelovich, *New Rules,* pp. xviii, 13–14, 34–35; also my discussion, p. 41.

23. Robert N. Bellah, Richard Madsen, William M. Sullivan, Ann Swidler, and Steven M. Tipton, *Habits of the Heart: Individualism and Commitment in American Life* (Berkeley, 1985).

3. Matters Arising

1. David Riesman, with Nathan Glazer, *Faces in the Crowd: Individual Studies in Character and Politics* (New Haven, 1950).

2. Max Lerner, *America as a Civilization* (New York, 1957), ch. 9, sec. 4 ("Varieties of American Character").

3. Christopher Lasch, *The Culture of Narcissism: American Life in an Age of Diminishing Expectations* (New York, 1979), pp. 90–91, 390–91; cf. pp. 74–75 in the Warner paperback. A searching historical and psychological review of Lasch's thesis by Jesse F. Battan does not fully expose his ambiguity on the prevalence of narcissism but examines at length the evidence for and against the proposition that clinical narcissism and related "character disorders" have

increased. Battan, "The 'New Narcissism' in 20th-Century America: The Shadow and Substance of Social Change,"*Journal of Social History* 17 (1983), pp. 199–220. In the main, I am leaving references on the validity of social-character theories to this book's sequel: Wilkinson, ed., *American Social Character*.

4. Daniel Yankelovich, *New Rules: Searching for Self-Fulfillment in a World Turned Upside Down* (New York, 1981), pp. 58–62, 78–84, based on a 1979 survey plus case examples. Of the studies reviewed here so far, only Yankelovich and Lipset (pp. 24–25, 35–37) used statistical surveys extensively, and only Lipset used them to make international comparisons. But see also Joseph Veroff et al., pp. 43–44.

5. David Riesman, writing ten years after *The Lonely Crowd* but twenty years before his piece on "Egocentrism," claimed that Americans were more sociable in conversations outside their families "than at any earlier time." Riesman et al., "Sociability, Permissiveness, and Equality," *Psychiatry* 23 (November 1960), pp. 323–40, reprinted in David Riesman, *Abundance for What? and Other Essays* (New York, 1964): see p. 190 in the Anchor paperback, referring to John W. Riley, "Dynamics of Non-Family Leisure in a New England Town" (Ph.D. diss., Social Relations, Harvard University, 1937).

6. Melvin L. Kohn, "Bureaucratic Man: A Portrait and an Interpretation," *American Sociological Review* 36 (1971), pp. 461–74. Kohn also claimed that work was more complex in large organizations, which encouraged intellectual flexibility. Kohn controlled for education and for government/nongovernment organizations, and his findings held for a wide range of job levels; but he tended to tap for a more rigid conformity than Whyte envisaged. For Whyte's own survey results supporting his thesis, see *The Organization Man* (New York, 1956), pp. 76–77 in the Simon and Schuster Clarion paperback. Complex support for Whyte's position can also be found in Carol Z. Stearns and Peter N. Stearns, *Anger: The Struggle for Emotional Control in America's History* (Chicago, 1986), ch. 5.

7. On the decline of anti-intellectualism and the growth of sensitivity, see Rupert Wilkinson, *American Tough: The Tough-Guy Tradition and American Character* (Westport, 1984; New York, 1986), pp. 103–4, 107–10. On changes in child-rearing values, see Alex Inkeles, "The American Character," *Center Magazine* 16 (November–December 1983), citing the Detroit Area Study.

8. The term 'yuppie' was used to describe supporters of Gary Hart in 1984. It is sometimes confused with Young Upwardly Mobile Professional (yumpie). Yuppies do strive upward, but frequently they are upper-middle-class to begin with. Cf. *Oxford English Dictionary, Supplement,* vol. IV; Marissa Piesman and Marilee Hartley, *The Yuppie Handbook: The State-of-the-Art Manual for Young Urban Professionals* (New York, 1984). The term reflects the 'gen-

trification' of some inner-city areas, a trend that is not confined to the U.S. but has not, as yet, reversed movements to the suburbs and beyond. See Kenneth T. Jackson, *Crabgrass Frontier: The Suburbanization of the United States* (New York, 1985), pp. 8, 302–3; Neil Smith and Peter Williams, eds., *Gentrification of the City* (Boston, 1986).

9. Jackson (note 8 above), ch. 15; also picture caption on shopping malls following p. 250. Cf. Bennett Berger, *Working-Class Suburb: A Study of Auto Workers in Suburbia* (Berkeley, 1960).

10. Joseph Veroff, Elizabeth Douvain, and Richard Kulka, *The Inner American: A Self-Portrait from 1957 to 1976* (New York, 1981). The 1976 survey also added some new questions. The findings are partly summarized by Carin Rubinstein, "The Revolution Within," *Psychology Today* (August 1981), pp. 78–81. David Halle's study of New Jersey chemical workers suggests that Veroff et al. overlooked informal communities at work, though Halle argues that social security and other factors have reduced interdependence: Halle, *America's Working Man: Work, Home, and Politics Among Blue-Collar Property Owners* (Chicago, 1984), pp. 47–48, 50–51, 314. On communities of interdependence among poor black women, see Carol Stack, *All Our Kin: Strategies for Survival in a Black Community* (New York, 1974).

11. Yearning for the inherited community is most explicit in Paul Wachtel, *The Poverty of Affluence: A Psychological Portrait of the American Way of Life* (New York, 1983). An opposite view, like mine above but less qualified, is that of Peter Clecak, *America's Quest for the Ideal Self: Dissent and Fulfillment in the '60s and '70s* (New York, 1983). Clecak believes that Americans often seek "personal fulfillment . . . within one or more communities of valued others."

12. Cf. Halle (note 10 above), pp. 169–70; Inkeles (note 7 above), pp. 30–31. Paul Kennedy, "The (Relative) Decline of America," *Atlantic Monthly* 260 (August 1987), pp. 29–38, lucidly summarizes the U.S. economy's mixture of decline and dynamism; he notes its comparatively high "labor mobility" and its many "new entrepreneurs."

13. In Sinclair Lewis, *Babbitt* (1922), one of Chum Frink's poems gives a splendid description of consumer goods and facilities as a social currency away from home: see ch. 14, sec. 3.

14. The phrase is from Florence King, "The Niceness Factor: Good Guyism in America," *Harper's Magazine* (October 1981), pp. 60–64.

15. See David C. McClelland, *The Roots of Consciousness* (Princeton, 1964), ch. 4; cf. McClelland, *The Achieving Society* (Princeton, 1961); and Gabriel A. Almond and Sidney Verba, *The Civic Culture: Political Attitudes and Democracy in Five Nations* (Princeton, 1963), pp. 169ff., 301ff. High American membership in voluntary associations was mainly due to (1) high membership rates among American women; (2) a large proportion of college-edu-

cated people (who tend to join associations more) in the U.S. population; (3) relatively high membership rates among lower-class people in America. See tables, ibid., pp. 302–4. The other nations compared were Britain, West Germany, Italy, and Mexico.

16. See also Frances FitzGerald, *Cities on a Hill: A Journey through Contemporary American Culture* (New York, 1986).

17. See especially Whyte's superbly written ch. 26 ("The Outgoing Life") in *The Organization Man* (New York, 1956).

18. See David Riesman et al., *The Lonely Crowd: A Study of the Changing American Character* (New Haven, 1950), ch. 13; and Whyte (note 17 above), p. 395 in the Simon and Schuster Clarion paperback.

19. Potter's article on American women cited comments from the 1950s on consumption pressures and female identity; cf. pp. 21–22 above; also Betty Friedan, *The Feminine Mystique* (New York, 1963).

20. Whyte's observations on social science and control in *The Organization Man* are on pp. 27, 29, 40 of the Clarion paperback.

21. On the survival of craftsmanship amid consumer other-direction, see Riesman et al. (note 18 above), ch. 15. My view of the continuity in Riesman's beliefs is partly based on periodic conversations with him from the 1960s to the 1980s.

22. Margaret Mead, *And Keep Your Powder Dry: An Anthropologist Looks at America* (New York, 1942), chaps. 8, 10.

23. Daniel Horowitz, *The Morality of Spending: Attitudes Toward the Consumer Society, 1875–1940* (Baltimore, 1985). Not all the positions were unfavorable: see, for example, Simon N. Patten, *The New Basis of Civilization* (New York, 1907).

24. Four of the studies looked back in this way: those by William Whyte (1956), Charles Reich (1970), David Riesman (1980), and Robert Bellah et al. (1985). Christopher Lasch looked for social responsibility more to the pre-Revolutionary "Puritan": *The Culture of Narcissism* (1979), ch. 3.

25. Vance Packard was also an author of two earlier books: *How to Pick a Mate: The Guide to Happy Marriage,* with Clifford Adams (New York, 1946), beamed at the post–World War II market; and *Animal I.Q.: The Human Side of Animals* (New York, 1950).

26. Vance Packard, *The Waste Makers* (New York, 1960), ch. 20 ("The Changing American Character"); also chaps. 1, 18. Packard quoted the phrase "new softness" from Dr. Eugene Kincaid's controversial report on the behavior of American POWs in Korea. Cf. H. H. Wubben, "American Prisoners of War in Korea," *American Quarterly* 22 (1970), pp. 3–19.

27. See Ralph Barton Perry, *Characteristically American* (New York, 1949), ch. 1; David Potter, "American Individualism in the Twentieth Century," in Gordon Mills, ed., *Innocence and Power: Individualism in Twentieth-Century*

America (1965), pp. 109–12; Seymour Martin Lipset, *The First New Nation* (New York, 1963), ch. 3.

28. In the following list, F means 'mainly favorable,' IU 'intentionally unfavorable,' EU 'effectively (but maybe unintentionally) unfavorable,' and MN 'mixed or neutral.' Two studies that end by observing new, favorable trends are still mainly unfavorable: Riesman (1980) and Yankelovich (1981). My classification is: Mead, *And Keep Your Powder Dry* (1942), MN; Gorer, *American People* (1948), EU; Laski, *American Democracy* (1949), F; Perry, chapter in *Characteristically American* (1949), F; Riesman et al., *Lonely Crowd* (1950), EU; Potter, *People of Plenty* (1954), MN; Whyte, *Organization Man* (1956), IU; Lerner, chapter in *America as a Civilization* (1957), EU; Packard, chapter in *Waste Makers* (1960), IU: Potter, essays (1962–63), MN; Lipset, "Changing American Character?" (1963), F; Pierson, essays (1954–64), MN; Henry, *Culture Against Man* (1963), IU; Reich, *Greening of America* (1970), MN; Slater, *Pursuit of Loneliness* (1970), IU; Lewis, *Culture of Inequality* (1978), IU; Lasch, *Culture of Narcissism* (1979), IU; Riesman, "Egocentrism" (1980), IU; Yankelovich, *New Rules* (1981), IU; Veroff et al., *Inner American* (1981), MN; Bellah et al., *Habits of the Heart* (1985), IU. As this list shows, interpretations of American character became more consistently and explicitly critical after the 1960s. If one adds to the total list a small number of more minor or specialized studies of American character not covered in the text, the result is slightly more balanced but not much.

29. Almond and Verba (note 15 above), p. 102. The other four countries were Britain, West Germany, Italy, and Mexico.

30. In the early 1900s, the British Liberal statesman Charles Masterman wrote a brilliant account of the way rich Wall Streeters enjoyed and even purchased spiritual criticism—and then returned to "the Stock Exchange gamble": C. F. G. Masterman, *The Condition of England* (London, 1909), pp. 31–32. Richard Hofstadter, *Anti-intellectualism in American Life* (New York, 1963), pp. 418–19, applied a somewhat similar analysis to the appetite of bourgeois Americans for jeremiads of their character and society, though he saw this as a new development.

4. Community

1. Kathy E. Ferguson, *The Feminist Case Against Bureaucracy* (Philadelphia, 1984), pp. 197–98. The statement by John Lewis, on his experience as a young black civil rights leader in the 1960s, is from an interview printed in William Beardslee, ed., *The Way Out Must Lead On* (Westport, 1983). I am grateful to Vivien Hart and Richard King for these references.

2. In a subtle and wide-ranging, but obscurely argued essay, Michael Zuckerman attributed a new dualism between individualism and community to complex forces of "modernization." Zuckerman, "The Fabrication of Iden-

tity in Early America," *William and Mary Quarterly* 34 (1977), 3d ser., pp. 183–214. In their section on individualism and community in American history, Robert Bellah et al. discuss two of the cases I do—Winthrop's Puritanism and Benjamin Franklin—but they do not really get into the connections between individualism and affiliation; and their subsequent references to Progressivism (another of my cases) are oversimplified. See Bellah et al., *Habits of the Heart: Individualism and Commitment in American Life* (Berkeley, 1985), ch. 2 and pp. 209–10, 261–62. Arthur M. Schlesinger, Sr., "Biography of a Nation of Joiners," *American Historical Review* 50 (1944–45), pp. 1–15, does survey American history for the 'joining' aspects of individualism, but he does not analyze different kinds of individualism, and he sees no tension between it and joining. His article is reprinted in Schlesinger, *Paths to the Present* (New York, 1949). Writing in 1918–20, the great Dutch historian, Johan Huizinga, did explore historically America's combination of "individualism and association"; he said little, in fact, about their connection but briefly noted a shared source in Calvinism. Huizinga, *America* (New York, 1972), Part I, ch. 1. I should add that my own account here does not distinguish between collective behavior (contact with a number of people simultaneously) and a community which supplies many 'one-on-one' contacts.

3. All six of the historical vignettes draw on selected writers but are my interpretation of individualism and community. On John Winthrop, Anne Hutchinson, and Congregationalist theology, I have relied most on Edmund S. Morgan, *The Puritan Dilemma: The Story of John Winthrop* (Boston, 1958); and Morgan, *The Puritan Family: Religion and Domestic Relations in 17th Century New England* (Boston, 1944; rev. ed., New York, 1966). On local communalism, Timothy H. Breen, "Persistent Localism: English Social Change and the Shaping of New England Institutions," *William and Mary Quarterly* 32 (1975), 3d ser., pp. 3–28; and Clifford Shipton, "The New England Frontier," *New England Quarterly* 10 (1937), pp. 25ff. On Anne Hutchinson's followers, Bernard Bailyn, *New England Merchants in the Seventeenth Century* (Cambridge, Mass., 1955), ch. 2; and Emory Battis, *Saints and Sectaries: Anne Hutchinson and the Antinomian Controversy in the Massachusetts Bay Colony* (Chapel Hill, 1962), ch. 17. On Salem, Marion Starkey, *The Devil in Massachusetts: A Modern Enquiry into the Salem Witch Trials* (New York, 1949); Paul Boyer and Stephen Nissenbaum, *Salem Possessed: The Social Origins of Witchcraft* (Cambridge, Mass., 1974); and John P. Demos, *Entertaining Satan: Witchcraft in the Culture of Early New England* (New York, 1982). Boyer and Nissenbaum argue that the idea of witchcraft was initially suggested to the girls by adults asking, "Who afflicted you?" On youthful high jinks, see Roger Thompson, "Adolescent Culture in Colonial Massachusetts," *Journal of Family History* 9 (1984), pp. 127–44, which used Middlesex County

Court records, 1649–99. My account, by definition, underplays the less influential, non-Puritan members of the early settlements. Zuckerman (note 2 above) gives a rather different analysis of individualism and community in Puritan New England.

4. *Dictionary of American Biography* (New York, 1931), vol. VI, pp. 585–98.

5. This section on Franklin was essentially written before I read Esmond Wright's biography, *Franklin of Philadelphia* (Cambridge, Mass., 1986). Wright's notion of Franklin's individualism is similar but not identical to mine: see Wright, p. 88. I have used Benjamin Franklin, *The Autobiography and Other Writings*, ed. Jesse Lemisch (New York, 1961). Cf. R. Jackson Wilson's literary interpretation in his introduction to the 1981 Modern College Library edition of *The Autobiography of Benjamin Franklin* (New York, 1981). According to Wilson, Franklin's own account portrayed an early drive for independence, followed in later life by association with others for mutual benefit. Kenneth Silverman's introduction to the 1986 Penguin edition of *The Autobiography and Other Writings* argues that, beneath his sociability, Franklin feared disappointment, distrusted others, and avoided intimacy. Silverman underestimates, I think, Franklin's friendships.

6. Cf. Paul E. Johnson, *A Shopkeeper's Millennium: Society and Revivals in Rochester, New York, 1815–1837* (New York, 1978), incl. tables on pp. 104, 106; Charles G. Finney, *Autobiography* (New York, 1876); Robert Samuel Fletcher, *History of Oberlin College* (Oberlin, 1943), vol. I, p. 18, quoting a firsthand account of Finney's 1830 sermon. Lyman Beecher's *Six Sermons: The Nature, Occasions . . . of Intemperance* (Boston, 1827), included the proposition that abstinence, not drinking, nurtured "the full flow of social affection" (pp. 22–23). On other aspects of pre–Civil War evangelical movements in relation to individualism and community, see esp. Paul Boyer, *Urban Masses and Moral Order in America, 1820–1920* (Cambridge, Mass., 1978); John L. Thomas, "Romantic Reform in America," *American Quarterly* 17 (1965), pp. 657–81; Julie Roy Jeffrey, *Frontier Women: The Trans-Mississippi West 1840–1880* (New York, 1979), ch. 6 (on the Mormons); Lawrence J. Friedman, *Gregarious Saints: Self and Community in American Abolitionism, 1830–1870* (New York, 1982). I am grateful to R. Jackson Wilson for some of my ideas on Charles Finney above.

7. Cf. Lillian Schlissel, ed., *Women's Diaries of the Westward Journey* (New York, 1982), esp. pp. 85–89; John Mack Faragher, *Women and Men on the Overland Trail* (New Haven, 1979). The Green and Jersey Company resolution is quoted by Daniel Boorstin, *The Americans: The National Experience* (New York, 1965), p. 66. Boorstin explores the myriad uses of cooperative organization on the supposedly individualistic frontier, but he stresses democracy rather than the more intimate aspects of community. Communal life

and work, particularly among men, is emphasized by John Mack Faragher, *Sugar Creek: Life on the Illinois Prairie* (New Haven, 1986), esp. ch. 14. Thomas Bender, *Community and Social Change in America* (New Brunswick, N.J., 1982), p. 96, briefly notes the overlap between "instrumental" and "communal" societies, with special reference to the West and to ethnic organization in the nineteenth century. On networks of female friendship and correspondence in the nineteenth century, see Carroll Smith Rosenberg, "The Female Role of Love and Ritual," *Signs* 1 (1975), pp. 1–30, reprinted in Linda K. Kerber and June De Hart, eds., *Women's America* (New York, 1982).

8. James Frear, *Forty Years of Progressive Public Service* (Washington, D.C., 1937), p. 248, is quoted by Valerie Watt, "Our Kind of Self: Autobiography and American Progressives" (Ph.D. diss., American Studies, University of Sussex, 1987), ch. 2. Watt explores other themes too, which entwine individualism and collectivism. "Language of social bonds" is quoted from Daniel T. Rodgers, "In Search of Progressivism," *Reviews in American History* 10 (1982), pp. 113–31. Other especially relevant studies and sources are Theodore P. Greene, *America's Heroes: The Changing Models of Success in American Magazines* (New York, 1970), chaps. 5, 6; Otis Graham, *Encore for Reform: The Old Progressives and the New Deal* (New York, 1967); Brand Whitlock, *Forty Years of It* (New York, 1914); Tom L. Johnson, *My Story* (Sterling, 1911); Jane Addams, *Twenty Years at Hull-House* (New York, 1910); and Allen F. Davis, *American Heroine: The Life and Legend of Jane Addams* (New York, 1973), esp. ch. 5.

9. Cf. Richard G. King, "Citizenship and Self-Respect: The Experience of Politics in the Civil Rights Movement, 1955–1965," *Journal of American Studies* 22 (April 1988). On the nineteenth century, see especially David Thelen, *Paths of Resistance: Tradition and Dignity in Industrializing Missouri* (New York, 1986), esp. introd., chaps. 9, 11. Thelen explores diverse communal resistances to large-scale capitalist developments; he is particularly interesting on the circles that many different people drew around their lives in the form of lodges and fraternities, though much more needs to be said on the appeal of their secret rituals.

10. Susan Porter Benson, "The Customers Ain't God," in Michael H. Frisch and Daniel J. Walkowitz, eds., *Working-Class America* (Urbana, 1983). Benson did not explore changes within the 1890–1940 period.

11. Cf. Benson (note 10 above); and "Rules and Regulations" for Siegel and Cooper employees, c. 1900, reprinted in David J. and Sheila M. Rothman, eds., *Sources of the American Social Tradition* (New York, 1975), vol. II, pp. 15–16. Also Roy Rosenzweig, *Eight Hours for What We Will: Workers and Leisure in an Industrial City, 1870–1920* (New York, 1983); David Halle, *America's Working Man: Work, Home and Politics Among Blue-Collar Property Owners* (Chicago, 1984), parts II, III.

12. On community and American federalism in the college consortium movement, see Rupert Wilkinson, "Lessons from the Valley of Cooperation," *Times Higher Education Supplement* (London, October 10, 1985).

13. I say more about this in an article on my own twenty-fifth reunion, "Harvard '61," *London Review of Books* 8 (November 20, 1986), pp. 20, 22. In the midst of reports exposing a decline in college history enrollments and widespread American ignorance of the country's basic history, Michael Kammen has shown that Americans' ignorance of their Constitution is not new either: Kammen, *A Machine That Would Go of Itself: The Constitution in American Culture* (New York, 1986); cf. Barbara Vobejda, on survey by National Endowment for the Humanities, *Washington Post* (September 1, 1987). But do other peoples do better? American national journalists and politicians refer to historical precedents and lessons, from the New Deal to the Vietnam War, much more than do their British counterparts.

14. My summary of traditional links between American individualism and affiliation (pp. 14–15, 25–26) builds on observations by Geoffrey Gorer and George Pierson. Alexis de Tocqueville, *Democracy in America* (London, 1835); James Truslow Adams, *The American: The Making of a New Man* (New York, 1943), p. 374; Schlesinger (note 2 above); Max Lerner, *America as a Civilization* (New York, 1957), vol. II, ch. 9, sec. 2 ("The Joiners"); Gabriel Almond and Sidney Verba, *The Civic Culture* (Princeton, 1963), esp. pp. 185, 302; David C. McClelland, *The Achieving Society* (Princeton, 1961) and *The Roots of Consciousness* (Princeton, 1964); Rupert Wilkinson, *American Tough: The Tough-Guy Tradition and American Character* (Westport, 1984; New York, 1986), ch. 3 ("Organized Individuals"). See also Huizinga (note 2 above); Garry Wills, *Reagan's America: Innocents at Home* (New York, 1987), chaps. 10, 41.

15. On regimentation and individualism in American football, see Wilkinson (note 14 above), pp. 80–81, 160, which, however, underestimates the average player's range of choice on the field. On community and class in local football, I am indebted to Larry Jacobs, ex–football player and political scientist.

5. Four Fears (I)

1. Barbara T. Roessner's article, which also appeared in the *International Herald Tribune* (October 20, 1986) as "Teach Pampered Children a Sense of Moral Purpose," took up the claim by Robert Coles that prep school students lacked social concern and shared purpose, contrasting with the "moral sensibility" of small southern black children in the civil rights crisis of the 1960s.

2. Mary Rowlandson, *A Narrative of the Captivity and Restauration of Mrs Mary Rowlandson* (1682), reprinted in, e.g., Frederick W. Turner III, ed., *The Portable North American Reader* (New York, 1973), pp. 312–59; Kurt Von-

negut, *Slaughterhouse Five, or, the Children's Crusade* (New York, 1970). Stephen Fender sees in the theme of capture an initiation rite one must go through to rejoin one's fellows or become truly American. Fender, "The Enemy Within," BBC Radio 3 broadcast (July 4, 1987). See also Tony Tanner, *City of Words: American Fiction, 1950–1970* (London, 1971); Rupert Wilkinson, "Connections with Toughness: The Novels of Eugene Burdick," *Journal of American Studies* 11 (1977), pp. 235–36. Like me, Fender and Tanner have the comparative perspective of being British-based.

3. Charlotte Erickson, *Invisible Immigrants: The Adaptation of English and Scottish Immigrants in Nineteenth-Century America* (London, 1972); Ely Chinoy, *Automobile Workers and the American Dream* (Boston, 1955), ch. 7; Rowland Berthoff, "Independence and Enterprise: Small Business in the American Dream," in Stuart W. Bruchey, ed., *Small Business in American Life* (New York, 1980); David Halle, *America's Working Man: Work, Home and Politics Among Blue-Collar Property Owners* (Chicago, 1984); Carl Degler, *At Odds: Women and the Family in America from the Revolution to the Present* (New York, 1980), esp. pp. 371–73. Hugh Brogan has noted that the widespread wish of black freedmen after the Civil War to have their own land was true to Jeffersonian political economy, though seldom recognized as such. Brogan, *Pelican History of the U.S.A.* (New York, 1986), p. 369.

4. Michael Maccoby, *The Gamesman: The New Corporate Leaders* (New York, 1976), pp. 93, 190; and, e.g., Wayne Dyer, *Pulling Your Own Strings* (New York, 1978). Bob Hoffman, *No One Is to Blame: Getting a Loving Divorce from Mom and Dad* (Palo Alto, 1979), offers a deeper therapy aimed at getting adults out of thralldom to early relationships with their parents. See Rupert Wilkinson, *American Tough: The Tough-Guy Tradition and American Character* (Westport, 1984; New York, 1986), pp. 72, 156, for more on such literature and on Maccoby's findings in relation to Riesman's "other-direction." For a different view of the fear of corporate and professional "entrapment," see Christopher Lasch, *The Culture of Narcissism: American Life in an Age of Diminishing Expectations* (New York, 1979), p.93n in the Warner paperback.

5. Quoted by Richard Sennett and Jonathan Cobb, *The Hidden Injuries of Class* (New York, 1972). On Harvard men's occupations, the sources of my data were the autobiographical *Class Reports* of the Harvard Class of 1961: the tenth and twenty-fifth anniversary editions (Cambridge, Mass., 1971, 1986). Cf. Rupert Wilkinson, "Harvard '61," *London Review of Books* 8 (November 20, 1986), p. 20.

6. The Declaration of Sentiments, agreed at the Seneca Falls Convention, July 19–20, 1848, was written by Elizabeth Cady Stanton, and is reprinted in, e.g., Linda K. Kerber and Jane De Hart Mathews, *Women's America: Refocusing the Past* (New York, 1982), pp. 431–33. The convention and subsequent ones in the 1860s drew analogies between female "bondage" and black slavery, for

black as well as white women. Cf. Stanton et al., eds., *A History of Woman Suffrage* (New York, 1882), vol. II, esp. pp. 193–94, 382–92. On resistance to marriage in the late nineteenth and early twentieth centuries, see Degler (note 3 above), pp. 159–65. Among modern manuals for women's independence, see Stanlee Phelps and Nancy Austin, *The Assertive Woman* (San Luis Obispo, 1975); Susan Forward with Joan Torres, *Men Who Hate Women and Women Who Love Them* (New York, 1986); cf. Sonya Friedman, *Smart Cookies Don't Crumble: A Modern Woman's Guide to Living and Loving Her Life* (New York, 1985); Howard Halpern, *How to Break Your Addiction to a Person* (New York, 1982).

7. Lasch (note 4 above) and David Riesman, "Egocentrism: Is the American Character Changing?" *Encounter* 55 (August-September 1980), pp. 19–28, explicitly referred to the first, atomistic type of literature. As I have already said, however, these and other social-character works of the seventies and eighties also expressed their own types of fear of being owned.

8. See Benjamin DeMott, "Threats and Whimpers: The New Business Heroes," *New York Times Book Review* (October 26, 1986), pp. 1, 49–51, on two types of hero in contemporary popular business literature.

9. Arthur M. Schlesinger, Jr., *A Thousand Days: John F. Kennedy in the White House* (Boston, 1965), ch. 27, sec. 2.

10. Ellen Goodman, "Gathered in Like the Sheaves of a Ritual Family Harvest," *International Herald Tribune* (December 2, 1986), p. 5.

11. Stephan Thernstrom, *A History of the American People,* 2 vols. (New York, 1984), p. viii in both volumes. On a more arcane level, the profusion of cyclical and other theories of change in American history and politics may reflect a wish to contain, in the mind at least, a sprawling society; to connect experiences that would otherwise seem horribly disjunctive.

12. Studs Terkel, *American Dreams: Lost and Found* (New York, 1980), ch. 1. Daniel Snowman has suggested that what I would call the fear of winding down is a carryover from the Puritan need to keep on doing better to show one was blessed. Snowman, *Britain and America: An Interpretation of British and American Culture 1945–1975* (New York, 1977), pp. 43–44, 51–52.

13. Quoted by James David Barber, *Presidential Character: Predicting Performance in the White House* (New York, 1972), pp. 348, 353. Cf. Richard M. Nixon, *Six Crises* (New York, 1968).

14. William J. Lederer and Eugene Burdick, *The Ugly American* (New York, 1958). Cf. Wilkinson (note 2 above), pp. 231–32. Burdick himself was a compulsive achiever.

15. Srully Blotnick, *The Corporate Steeplechase: Predictable Crises in a Business Career* (Baltimore, 1984); Stephen Burglas, *The Success Syndrome: Hitting Bottom When You Reach the Top* (New York, 1986); Judith Viorst, *Necessary Losses* (New York, 1986).

16. Ronald Reagan, Inaugural Address (January 21, 1985). Or again, on 'Irangate': "let it never be said of this generation of Americans that we became so obsessed with failure that we refused to take risks that could further the cause of peace and freedom." Reagan, State of the Union Address (January 27, 1987). Consider also the wistful/hopeful note in the banner book ad for the autobiography of the famous pilot General Chuck Yeager: "YEAGER. HE SHOWED US HOW FAR AMERICA CAN GO." *New York Times Book Review* (July 14, 1985), p. 8.

17. Judith M. Bardwick, *The Plateauing Trap: How to Avoid It in Your Career . . . and Your Life* (New York, 1986). On the demographic and social background, see Eli Ginzberg and George Vojta, *Beyond Human Scale: The Large Corporation at Risk* (New York, 1985).

18. Examples of such writing are Gail Sheehy's best-selling *Passages: Predictable Crises of Adult Life* (New York, 1976), esp. ch. 1; James Fallows, "Possibilities," *Atlantic Monthly* (November 1985); David Owen, "Pfft," *Atlantic Monthly* (December 1985). Also Tennessee Williams's play *Sweet Bird of Youth* (1959), whose banal closing words about "the enemy, time in us all" do not match its subtler uses of that theme throughout. For other perspectives on the fear of aging in America, see David Hackett Fischer, *Growing Old in America* (New York, 1977); Lasch (note 4 above), passim; Wilkinson (note 4 above), pp. 91, 164; Garry Wills, *Reagan's America: Innocents at Home* (New York, 1987), pp. 1–4; Robert J. Samuelson, "The Middle-Aging of America May Not Be Born," *International Herald Tribune* (July 31, 1987).

19. See Jeff Meyer's article, *Los Angeles Times* (May 14, 1986), printed as "Fitness Standards Slump for U.S. Children" in *International Herald Tribune* (same date). Cf. John F. Kennedy, "The Soft American," *Sports Illustrated* (December 26, 1960), reprinted in John Talamani and Charles H. Page, eds., *Sport and Society: An Anthology* (Boston, 1973).

20. Harvey Green, *Fit for America: Health, Fitness, Sport and American Society* (New York, 1986), also claims that personal cults of physical fitness often compensated for failure in a society where, by definition, few could win. An unexpected trace of the fear of winding down and the fear of falling away crosses the pages of Lee Iacocca and William Novak's top-selling *Iacocca—An Autobiography* (New York, 1984). Fired at fifty-three by Henry Ford II, then saving the near-bust Chrysler, symbol of U.S. industrial worries, Iacocca deals more reassuringly with the fear of winding down than with that of falling away. As he presents it, he operates successfully but disapprovingly in a "bull-shitting" society, hooked on TV and credit-card debt, a far cry from the familial and frugal, pay-as-you-earn society he grew up in.

21. Jerry Falwell, *Listen, America!* (New York, 1980). On lack of purpose and common values, Falwell was pleased to quote the historian Eugene Genovese, without saying (or realizing?) that he was a Marxist! (p. 14).

22. *New York Times*/CBS poll reported in *New York Times* (November 25, 1985). Admittedly all percentages were minorities, and 'moderate,' too, won consistent pluralities, but much higher ones supported 'progressive': 37 percent favorable, 7 percent unfavorable in the whole sample. Most reactions presumably were neutral or 'don't knows,' owing to political ignorance or dislike of abstract labels.

23. Letter to Thomas Jefferson (December 11, 1819), in Lester J. Cappon, ed., *The Adams–Jefferson Letters* (Chapel Hill, 1959), vol. II, p. 549.

24. John F. Kennedy, "We Must Climb to the Hilltop," *Life* (September 26, 1960).

25. John Winthrop, "A Modell of Christian Charity" (1630), reprinted in Daniel Boorstin, ed., *An American Primer* (Chicago, 1966), vol. I, p. 22.

26. On New England Puritans and the loss of an English audience, see Perry Miller, *Errand into the Wilderness* (Cambridge, Mass., 1956). My notion of a historic American fear of falling away is influenced by Marcus Cunliffe, "American Watersheds," *American Quarterly* 13 (1961), pp. 480–94, and is similar to the thesis of Sacvan Bercovitch, *The American Jeremiad* (Madison, 1978). See also Bercovitch, "The Rites of Assent: Rhetoric, Ritual, and the Ideology of the American Consensus," in Sam B. Girgus, ed., *The American Self: Myth, Ideology, and Popular Culture* (Albuquerque, 1981). Bercovitch, however, virtually abandons the fearful side of American mission as he takes his story into the second half of the nineteenth century, and his two studies cited above have almost nothing specific on the twentieth century. I also believe that he overstresses the expansionist side of colonial Puritanism and the Puritan sources of the Revolution.

27. In his study of midwesterners, Harvey Varenne found more than I have that Americans ascribe the attainment of "real community [to a] golden age of early frontier days or seventeenth-century New England": Varenne, *Americans Together: Structured Diversity in a Midwestern Town* (New York, 1977), pp. 150–51. In declaring the frontier experience to be the key to American democracy, energy, and distinctiveness, Frederick Jackson Turner absorbed much of the American Revolution and the Constitutional period into it by stressing the populist demands of frontier counties in the eighteenth and early nineteenth centuries. Turner, "Contributions of the West to American Democracy" (1920), reprinted in George Rogers Taylor, ed., *The Turner Thesis: Problems in American Civilization* (Boston, 1956), pp. 21ff. Cf. Richard Maxwell Brown, "Back Country Rebellions and the Homestead Ethic in America, 1740–1799," in Brown and Don E. Fehrenbacher, eds., *Tradition, Conflict and Modernization: Perspectives on the American Revolution* (New York, 1977).

28. On the primacy of the American Revolution itself in elite American views of the national history, see Michael G. Kammen, "The American Rev-

olution in National Tradition," in Brown and Fehrenbacher, ibid.; Kammen, *A Season of Youth: The American Revolution in the Historical Imagination* (New York, 1978). The fear of falling away finds room for two notions of America's founding tradition: 'Lockean' property individualism and 'republican civic humanism.' A superbly written essay on this is Richard G. King, "Politics and the Self," *Over Here: An American Studies Journal* (University of Nottingham, England, October 1986), pp. 24–33, reviewing John P. Diggins, *The Lost Soul of American Politics* (New York, 1984) and Christopher Lasch, *The Minimal Self* (New York, 1985). For other relevant aspects of the Revolution and the Constitutional period in American political culture, see Robert N. Bellah, "Civil Religion in America," *Daedalus* 96 (Winter 1967), pp. 1–21; Rowland Berthoff, "Peasants and Artisans, Puritans and Republicans: Personal Liberty and Communal Equality in American History," *Journal of American History* 69 (1982–83), pp. 579–98.

29. Franklin D. Roosevelt, speech accepting renomination for President, Democratic National Convention (June 27, 1936), reprinted in Roosevelt, *Public Papers and Addresses,* ed. Samuel I. Rosenman (New York, 1938), vol. V, pp. 230–38; Richard M. Nixon, speech accepting nomination for President, Republican National Convention (August 8, 1968), reprinted in Arthur M. Schlesinger, Jr., and Fred Israel, eds., *History of American Presidential Elections* (New York, 1985), vol. IX, pp. 3832–40. On American founding virtues betrayed, see also the speech by the 'Radio Priest,' the Reverend Charles E. Coughlin (June 19, 1936), in Schlesinger and Israel, ibid., vol. VII, pp. 2866–77.

30. Martin Luther King, Jr., address at the March on Washington, *SCLC Newsletter* (September 1963), reprinted in August Meier et al., eds., *Black Protest Thought in the Twentieth Century* (Indianapolis, 1965), pp. 346–51 in 1971 rev. ed. Cf. Staughton Lynd, *The Intellectual Origins of American Radicalism* (Cambridge, Mass., 1968). According to Sacvan Bercovitch and Sam B. Girgus, American social and political critics have found it hard to avoid arguing in terms of an American tradition betrayed. See Bercovitch, "The Rites of Assent" (note 26 above), and Girgus, *The New Covenant: Jewish Writers and the American Idea* (Chapel Hill, 1984), esp. pp. 10–15, based on Bercovitch's thesis. Bercovitch notes the controlling and unifying function of Revolutionary myth in a society of "marketplace" individualism.

31. I explore rhetoric related to all four fears in a study of the national convention acceptance speeches of Democratic and Republican nominees for President, 1948–80: Wilkinson, "Saying Yes," *London Review of Books* (July 19–August 1, 1984), pp. 18ff., which notes among other things a paradoxical praise of geographical diversity and the doughtiness of rivals to establish national and party unity; and a backward- yet forward-looking concern with national decline, restoration, and greatness.

32. Andrew Jackson's famous message of July 10, 1832, defending his veto of the bill to recharter the national Bank of the United States, made much of the distinction between "natural" inequalities of talent and reward, and "artificial" (European-like) ranks and privileges. See the speech in Richard Hofstadter, ed., *Great Issues in American History: From the Revolution to the Civil War, 1765–1865* (New York, 1958), esp. p. 294. Roderick Nash, *Wilderness and the American Mind* (New Haven, 1967; rev. ed., 1973), chaps. 1–4, brilliantly documents the tension between pastoral and primitivist views of nature in early America, and their sources in ancient and European history. Cf. Ray Allen Billington, *Land of Savagery, Land of Promise: The European Image of the American Frontier in the Nineteenth Century* (New York, 1981); John William Ward, *Andrew Jackson—Symbol for an Age* (New York, 1953); Fred Somkin, *Unquiet Eagle: Memory and Desire in the Idea of American Freedom, 1815–1860* (Ithaca, 1967), ch. 3 ("No Home on the Range"); Michael P. Rogin, "Nature as Politics and Nature as Romance in America," *Political Theory* 5 (1977), pp. 5–30. Bernard Bailyn, *The Ideological Origins of the American Revolution* (Cambridge, Mass., 1967), pp. 83ff., explores the colonial American notion that "America was a purer and freer England" and thus more natural. He attributes the idea to local Puritanism as well as European Enlightenment thought.

33. Daniel Webster, speech (August 28, 1847), in Webster, *Writings and Speeches* (New York, 1903), vol. IV, pp. 107–11. Leo Marx, *The Machine in the Garden: The Pastoral Ideal in America* (New York, 1964), pp. 209–15, analyzes other, related aspects of the speech. At one point in it, Webster presented the railroad as a violator of nature, but as Leo Marx noted, he did this mainly to spoof and belittle such a specter. Cf. Edward Everett, "On the Importance of Scientific Knowledge," speech to mechanics institutes, in Everett, *Orations and Speeches for Various Occasions* (Boston, 2d ed., 1850), vol. I, pp. 246ff. Everett, a polymathic public figure (orator, cleric, academic, politician), saw the growth of a magnificent manufacturing society based on the bounties of "Nature" and social liberties.

34. F. J. Turner, "The Significance of the Frontier in American History" (1893), reprinted in George Rogers Taylor, ed., *The Turner Thesis* (Boston, 1956), pp. 1–2. The 'reaper' analogy is mine. Turner quoted a politician from western Virginia who declared in 1830 that migrants to the West were "regenerated [by the] energy which the mountain breeze and western habits impart": ibid., p. 15. On the language of rebirth and renewal in modern presidential campaigns, see Wilkinson (note 31 above).

35. In the 1920s, advertisers ushered in consumer technology by presenting it as part of a natural or authentic progression. Cf. Roland Marchand, *Advertising the American Dream: Making Way for Modernity, 1920–1940* (Berkeley, 1985), esp. p. 129; David Nye, *Image Worlds: Corporate Identities at*

General Electric, 1890–1930 (Cambridge, Mass., 1985). David Shih, *The Simple Life: Plain Living and High Thinking in American Culture* (New York, 1985), explores naturalistic movements and yearnings in American history, and finds them to be mainly upper and upper middle class. Cf. John Herbers, *The New Heartland: America's Flight Beyond the Suburbs and How It Is Changing Our Future* (New York, 1986). A lower-class form of 'natural man' ideology is brilliantly suggested in Elliott J. Gorn's cultural study, "The Manassa Mauler and the Fighting Marine: An Interpretation of the Dempsey-Tunney Fights," *Journal of American Studies* 19 (1985), pp. 27–47. On political and other uses of the country boy—sometimes quite ambiguous—see Roger Butterfield, "The Folklore of Politics," *Pennsylvania Magazine of History and Biography* 74 (1950), pp. 164–77; William Burlie Brown, *The People's Choice: The Presidential Image in the Campaign Biography* (Baton Rouge, 1960); R. Richard Wohl, "The 'Country Boy' Myth and Its Place in Urban Culture," *Perspectives in American History* 3 (1969), pp. 77–156. Writing on *Crocodile Dundee* in the *New York Times* (January 17, 1987), Aljean Harmetz noted the popularity of 'fish out of water' movies, where the hero successfully copes with a ridiculously alien culture. By bringing together different backgrounds, such movies, I suggest, assuage the fear of falling apart.

36. Karen Haltunen, *Confidence Men and Painted Women: A Study of Middle-Class Culture in America, 1830–1870* (New Haven, 1982). After the Civil War, she noted, advice books put a new emphasis on 'magnetism' and handling people, along with economic self-help. In *Humbug: The Art of P. T. Barnum* (Boston, 1973), Neil Harris shows that antebellum Americans were fascinated with the mechanics of hoaxes, often based allegedly on natural wonders (from mermaids to moon men).

37. Owen Wister, *The Virginian: A Horseman of the Plains* (New York, 1902), "Rededication and Preface" (1911) and p. 16 in the 1956 Pocket Books paperback. More recently, the very titles of two of Robert Sklar's history books highlight an imposed, 'plastic' artificiality: *The Plastic Age: 1917–1930* (New York, 1970) and *Movie-Made America: A Cultural History of American Movies* (New York, 1975).

38. David Riesman, with Nathan Glazer and Reuel Denney, *The Lonely Crowd: A Study of the Changing American Character* (New Haven, 1950), chaps. 13, 15.

39. Joe McGinniss, *The Selling of the President 1968* (New York, 1969), pp. 36–37 in the 1970 Pocket Books paperback. The book's title is itself a phony—it is about the 'selling' of a presidential *candidate,* not then an incumbent.

40. Readers or viewers of *The Mosquito Coast* (novel by Paul Theroux, New York, 1981; movie with Harrison Ford, 1986) will remember that 'Have a nice day' becomes the bitter refrain of the mixed-up, back-to-nature protagonist,

Allie Fox, in his denunciations of a commercialized, inauthentic America. Cf. Theroux, *O-Zone* (New York, 1986).

41. Christopher Lasch, *The Culture of Narcissism: American Life in an Age of Diminishing Expectations* (New York, 1979), esp. p. 96 in the Warner paperback, and ch. 4; Daniel Boorstin, *The Image, or What Happened to the American Dream* (New York, 1962), reissued as *The Image: A Guide to Pseudo-Events in America* (New York, 1964), esp. p. 255 in the 1964 Harper paperback. Lasch briefly credited and discussed Boorstin: see Lasch (above), pp. 119, 142. On Ronald Reagan's own confusions of reality with fiction, propaganda, and myth, see Garry Wills, *Reagan's America: Innocents at Home* (New York, 1987).

42. Boorstin (note 41 above), pp. 259–61 in the Harper paperback. Although he mainly concentrated on America, some of his material was European, especially with regard to packaged travel. For other, more recent views of the blurring of reality in a capitalist, media-shaped society, see Arthur Miller's new 1984 ending to his play *The American Clock* (1980); and Todd Gitlin, ed., *Watching Television: A Pantheon Guide to Popular Culture* (New York, 1987). Cf. A. M. Rosenthal's op-ed article, *New York Times* (May 26, 1987), on "the surrogate life," from renting party hostesses to "surrogate motherhood."

6. Four Fears (II)

1. *The Memoirs of Capt. Roger Clapp* (written c.1680; printed, Boston, 1731) were reprinted in Alex Young, ed., *Chronicles of the First Planters of the Colony of Massachusetts Bay* (Boston, 1846). See p. 353 for the above quotation, and the following pages for a subtle mixture of grateful satisfaction and critical anxiety. Clapp ran military defenses for the colony.

2. Frederick Robinson, *An Oration Delivered Before the Trades Union of Boston and Vicinity* (Boston, 1834), p. 320 in the long abridgment by Joseph L. Blau, ed., *Social Theories of Jacksonian Democracy: Representative Writings of the Period, 1835–1850* (Indianapolis, 1954). Robinson was a Democratic state legislator and party leader in Massachusetts.

3. David Brion Davis, ed., *The Fear of Conspiracy: Images of Un-American Subversion from the Revolution to the Present* (Ithaca, 1971), gives other explanations of American conspiracy fear, though Davis's ideas overlap mine. See especially his comments on "the fear of betraying the priceless heritage won by the Founding Fathers," "the sense of an endangered national mission," and the use of conspiracy theories to summon Americans from prosperous lethargy: pp. xxii–xxiii in Davis's introduction. Cf. Richard Hofstadter, *The Paranoid Style in American Politics, and Other Essays* (New York, 1964), pp. 3–39. This study describes rather than giving causes. Both Davis and Hofstadter stress that exaggerations of conspiracy are no monopoly of Americans,

and both try to separate realistic fears and protests from fevered fantasies.

4. John Winthrop, "A Modell of Christian Charity" (1630), reprinted in Daniel Boorstin, ed., *An American Primer* (Chicago, 1966), vol. I, pp. 10–23.

5. Different strains within the election sermon and jeremiad tradition are explored by A. W. Plumstead, ed., *The Wall and the Garden: Selected Massachusetts Election Sermons, 1670–1775* (Minneapolis, 1968), and by Perry Miller, *The New England Mind: From Colony to Province* (Cambridge, Mass., 1953), chaps. 2, 3, which also documents resistance and alternatives to the jeremiad. Cf. Sacvan Bercovitch, *The American Jeremiad* (Madison, 1978), esp. introduction. On fears of decline and dissolution, see Joshua Scotow, *Old Men's Fears for Their Own Declensions Mixed with Fears of Their and Posterities Further Falling Off from New-England's Primitive Constitution* (Boston, 1691); Richard L. Bushman, *From Puritan to Yankee: Character and the Social Order in Connecticut, 1690–1765* (Cambridge, Mass., 1967), esp. ch. 4, including the issue of "outliving," moving away from the village and church center.

6. Cf. Plumstead (note 5 above), pp. 323ff.; Edmund S. Morgan, "The Puritan Ethic and the American Revolution," *William and Mary Quarterly* 24 (1967), pp. 4–43; Catherine L. Albanese, *Sons of the Fathers: The Civil Religion of the American Revolution* (Philadelphia, 1976). Plumstead attributes less fear of falling away to election sermons of the 1770s than his selection of sermons shows.

7. Bernard Bailyn, *The Ideological Origins of the American Revolution* (Cambridge, Mass., 1967), chaps. 2, 3. On the complex relation with black slavery, see Bailyn, pp. 232–46; Edmund S. Morgan, *American Slavery, American Freedom: The Ordeal of Colonial Virginia* (New York, 1975), pp. 375–76; George Washington (1774), in Davis (note 3 above), p. 34. The Declaration of Independence with Stephen Fender's commentary is in Fender, *American Literature in Context, I: 1620–1830* (London and New York, 1983), pp. 97–121. On the special American fear of arbitrary military power, see Bailyn, pp. 61ff.

8. George Washington's Farewell Address (1796) is reprinted in Boorstin (note 4 above), pp. 194–208. On enslavement by human passions, see Washington (above); Thomas Jefferson, *Notes on the State of Virginia* (1787), in Merrill D. Peterson, ed., *The Portable Thomas Jefferson* (New York, 1975), pp. 214–15; Albanese (note 6 above), pp. 29–30.

9. Cf. the brilliant essays by John F. Kasson, *Civilizing the Machine: Technology and Republican Values in America, 1776–1900* (New York, 1976), chaps. 1, 2. Also Daniel E. Shih, *The Simple Life: Plain Living and High Thinking in American Culture* (New York, 1985), chaps. 3, 4; Rupert Wilkinson, *American Tough: The Tough-Guy Tradition and American Character* (Westport, 1984; New York, 1986), pp. 46–47, 145. Revealing comments of the time include John Warren's July 4 *Oration* (1783), reprinted in Gordon S.

Wood, ed., *The Rising Glory of America: 1780–1820* (New York, 1971), pp. 55–69; and Royall Tyler's comedy *The Contrast: The American Son of Liberty* (1787), the first American play to be successfully performed by a professional company: reprinted in Richard Moody, ed., *Dramas from the American Theater, 1762–1909* (Cleveland, 1966), pp. 33ff.

10. On the similarities between rural preferences of some early textile manufacturers in England and America, I am indebted to an undergraduate paper by Jonathan Tutton, "A Comparison of Early Mass Production Development in England and the United States" (American Studies, University of Sussex, England, 1987). Tutton compared the early rural factory communities of Owen, Greg, Dale, and Arkwright in England (spanning from 1780 to 1820) with Lowell, Massachusetts, in the early nineteenth century. On both sides, Tutton noted the motive of getting a good supply of labor. The British took more responsibility for whole families and put more stress on outdoor health. Cf. Thomas Dublin, ed., *Farm and Factory: The Mill Experience and Women's Lives in New England, 1830–1860* (New York, 1981); also Anthony F. C. Wallace, *Rockdale: The Growth of an American Village in the Early Industrial Revolution* (New York, 1972), on developments in Pennsylvania.

11. Michael G. Kammen, "The American Revolution in National Tradition," in Richard Maxwell Brown and Don E. Fehrenbacher, eds., *Tradition, Conflict, and Modernization: Perspectives on the American Revolution* (New York, 1977), p. 24; cf. pp. 23–29. In his famous Bank Veto Message (July 10, 1832), Andrew Jackson claimed that special privileges given the rich by the Bank of the U.S. fomented political and personal conflict, a "fearful commotion" which threatened the Union. It was time to "revive that devoted patriotism and spirit of compromise which distinguished the sages of the Revolution and the fathers of our Union." Richard Hofstadter, ed., *Great Issues in American History: From the Revolution to the Civil War, 1765–1865* (New York, 1958), pp. 292, 295. Cf. George B. Forgie, *Patricide in the House Divided: A Psychological Interpretation of Lincoln and His Age* (New York, 1979).

12. See Fred Somkin, *Unquiet Eagle: Memory and Desire in the Idea of American Freedom, 1815–1860* (Ithaca, 1967), ch. 1, including the recurrent apocalyptic image of the volcano. (The salience of clergy and the 1840s–50s period in Somkin's sources of fearful statements is not remarked on by Somkin himself.) At a pioneers' reunion in 1859, Jim Matheny, local lawyer and civic leader, stated a very modern fear about losing community and related values in "the busy whirl of life." John Mack Faragher, *Sugar Creek: Life on the Illinois Prairie* (New Haven, 1986), pp. 222–25. Cf. John Higham, *From Boundlessness to Consolidation: The Transformation of American Culture, 1848–1860* (Ann Arbor, 1969); David Morse, *American Romanticism, vol. I, From Cooper to Hawthorne* (London, 1987), esp. p. 2.

13. Robinson (note 2 above), pp. 320–22.

14. On drinking and enslavement, see Lyman Beecher, *Six Sermons: The Nature, Occasions . . . of Intemperance* (Boston, 1827), pp. 6–9, 16, 48, 66; Heman Humphrey, "The Parallel Between Intemperance and the Slave Trade: An Address Delivered at Amherst College" (July 4, 1828), abridged in Walter E. Hugins, ed., *The Reform Impulse, 1825–1850* (New York, 1972), pp. 186–90. The Reverend Humphrey was president of Amherst. W. J. Rorabaugh, *The Alcoholic Republic: An American Tradition* (New York, 1979), supplies a wide-ranging background to drinking and its anxieties at the time. The political role of the fear of being owned could be seen in the anti-Masonic movement, attacking Freemasonry as a secret society which "enslaves the mind" (1830), and in Jackson's Bank Veto Message (1832) attacking the "present [of] the bounty of our government" to rich men and foreigners. See Davis (note 3 above), p. 78, and Hofstadter (note 11 above), pp. 291–92.

15. Text for a sermon by Reverend Elihu Baldwin of New York (1827), quoted by Somkin (note 12 above), p. 17. On Lincoln and depressive disorders in the western U.S., see Paul M. Angle, ed., *Abraham Lincoln's Speeches and Letters, 1832–1865* (New York, 1957), p. 17; cf. pp. 11, 30–32.

16. William Evans Arthur, *Oration* (Covington, Ky., 1850), is quoted at length and given a political and literary analysis by Bercovitch (note 5 above), pp. 145ff. Arthur, I must add, shifts his position on the Republic's resilience to deviations.

17. On the fear of encroachment and domination in Manifest Destiny policies, see Norman Graebner, ed., *Manifest Destiny* (Indianapolis, 1968), pp. xxxi, xlix. On other fears, Thomas R. Hietala, *Manifest Design: Anxious Aggrandizement in Late Jacksonian America* (Ithaca, 1985).

18. William Ellery Channing's argument, in a long letter-essay to Henry Clay (1837), is excerpted at length in Graebner, ed. (note 17 above), pp. 43–69. Full text is in *The Works of William E. Channing* (Boston, 1848), vol. II, pp. 184–248. In his own variation on Winthrop, Channing declared that America was sullying abroad "the cause of republicanism . . . In one respect, our institutions have disappointed us all. They have not wrought out for us that elevation of character, which is . . . the only substantial blessing of liberty." See Graebner, ed. (note 17 above), pp. 54, 55.

19. *New York Herald* (March 9, 1857), quoted by Bruce Catton, "The Dred Scott Case," in John A. Garraty, ed., *Quarrels That Have Shaped the Constitution* (New York, 1962), p. 89; Abraham Lincoln, speech against Kansas-Nebraska bill, Peoria, Ill. (October 16, 1854), in Angle, ed. (note 15 above), p. 58. Lincoln's sense of a falling away from Revolutionary principles and promise was not just rhetorical: see his letter to Prof. George Robertson (August 15, 1855), ibid., pp. 60–61. On northern attitudes to the South, see esp. Eric Foner, *Free Soil, Free Labor, Free Men: The Ideology of the Republican*

Party Before the Civil War (New York, 1970), chaps. 1–3; Mary Beth Norton et al., *A People and a Nation: A History of the United States* (Boston, 1982), vol. I, pp. 352 (cartoon), 354–55; Michael Feldman, "Rehearsal for the Civil War: Antislavery and Proslavery at the Fighting Point in Kansas, 1854–1856," in Lewis Perry and M. Feldman, eds., *Antislavery Reconsidered* (Baton Rouge, 1979).

20. On southern attitudes to the North, see esp. Stephen Channing, *Crisis of Fear: Secession in South Carolina* (New York, 1978), chaps. 1, 2; Norton et al. (note 19 above), p. 353; Foner (note 19 above), pp. 66–67; Feldman (note 19 above); Kenneth S. Greenberg, *Masters and Statesmen: The Political Culture of American Slavery* (Baltimore, 1985), ch. 5. Greenberg explores the southern ascription of "enslavement" to the North and the southern use of Revolutionary images. He argues that leading southerners enlisted an ambivalent Anglophobia in their hatred of northern power. Cf. John Tyler (1835), in Davis (note 3 above), pp. 140–43. On southern slavery expansionism, Eugene Genovese, *The Political Economy of Slavery: Studies in the Economy and Society of the Slave South* (New York, 1965), ch. 10, covers a wide range of motives and cites northern agreement that slavery must expand or die. See also Percy L. Rainwater, "Economic Benefits of Secession: Opinion in Mississippi in the 1850s," *Journal of Southern History* 1 (1935), pp. 459–74. David Herbert Donald, *Liberty and Union* (Lexington, Mass., 1975), pp. 72ff., gives a concise sense of deviations by various groups from the "dominant" attitudes in the North and South toward each other, but also notes the shift toward uniformity in the South.

21. Henry Ward Beecher, "The Advance of a Century," *Tribune*, Extra No. 33, Independence Day Orations (New York, July 4, 1876), reprinted in Alan Trachtenberg, ed., *Democratic Vistas, 1860–1880* (New York, 1970), pp. 67–72.

22. On the fear of losing local and personal autonomy, see Robert Wiebe, *The Search for Order: 1877–1920* (Chicago, 1967), ch. 3; and David Thelen, *Paths of Resistance: Tradition and Dignity in Industrializing Missouri* (New York, 1986), though at times Thelen may be imposing modern fears on his subjects. On "the two great classes—tramps and millionaires," see Ignatius Donnelly's magnificent preamble to the People's party platform, Omaha (July 4, 1892—no coincidence, that date), in Richard Hofstadter, ed., *Great Issues in American History, from Reconstruction to the Present Day* (New York, 1958; rev. ed., 1969), p. 148 in the Vintage paperback. Also George H. Martin, "New Standards of Patriotic Citizenship," *National Educational Proceedings* (1895), p. 137 and passim. On the 'second generation,' see Wilkinson (note 9 above), pp. 47–48, 146. On American urban industrial speedup and atomism, cf. William Dean Howells's parable of the millionaire Dryfoos in *A Hazard of New Fortunes* (New York, 1890), pp. 225–26 in the NAL Meridian paperback. Also

an interesting comparative observation by George Bernard Shaw, quoted by Daniel Aaron, *Men of Good Hope: A Story of American Progressives* (New York, 1951), p. 62; and Kasson (note 9 above), ch. 5.

23. Julius Grinnell (Chicago, 1886), quoted in Davis, ed. (note 3 above), p. 179. John Higham, "The Origins of Immigration Restriction, 1882–1897: A Social Analysis," *Mississippi Valley Historical Review* 39 (1952), pp. 77–88, discusses different phases and motives of anti-immigrant politics and stresses the fear of social chaos and class conflict. Jacob A. Riis's famous report, *How the Other Half Lives: Studies Among the Tenements of New York* (New York, 1890), demonstrated that concern about immigrants could involve fear of degeneracy and social explosion without leading to restrictionism, despair, or wholesale nativism.

24. Altgeld went on to give an 'underconsumptionist' view of what would befall "the great American market" if "the American laborer" was reduced to mere subsistence. Altgeld's address (Springfield, January 10, 1883) is reprinted in Henry M. Christman, ed., *The Mind and Spirit of John Peter Altgeld: Selected Writings and Addresses* (Urbana, 1960). It is a memorable speech for its combination of principles and concrete policies; its prescience on technological unemployment; and its assertion of a new interdependence between groups and classes.

25. On labor, immigrants, and left-wing attitudes, see Herbert G. Gutman, *Work, Culture and Society in Industrializing America* (New York, 1976), pp. 49–53. Cf. Henry Nash Smith, *Mark Twain's Fable of Progress: Political and Economic Ideas in* A Connecticut Yankee (New Brunswick, N.J., 1964), pp. 8–10. "Degenerating into European conditions" and other relevant phrases are in Donnelly's preamble to the 1892 Populist platform (note 22 above): ". . . the time has come when the railroad corporations must either own the people or the people must own the railroads." In *Distrust and Democracy: Political Distrust in Britain and America* (Cambridge, Eng., 1978), Vivien Hart has described the Populists as "exemplars of the continuing attempt in American politics to mix old values and new functions." Comparing Kansas Populists with working-class, radical democrats of Birmingham, England, in the same period, she shows that the Britons referred much less to past heroes, images, and traditions. When they did so, they felt they had to reach back far further to a vague "myth of Saxon democracy." Ibid., chaps. 3, 4, esp. pp. 148, 173.

26. Henry George, *Progress and Poverty* (privately printed, San Francisco, 1879; published, New York, 1880), expressed most obviously the fear of being owned by rentiers, but he also articulated fear of "petrifaction" and waste of energy through disunion, strife, and selfish inequality; a belief that civilization must either ascend to a "higher plane" or be "overwhelmed"; and a call to fulfill "letter and spirit" of the Declaration of Independence. See esp.

book 10 ("The Law of Human Progress"), which reflects the influence of Herbert Spencer and social Darwinism. On Frederick Law Olmsted's writing and influence between the 1850s and the early twentieth century, see Paul Boyer, *Urban Masses and Public Order in America, 1820–1920* (Cambridge, Mass., 1978), pp. 237–40. George M. Beard, *American Nervousness: Its Causes and Consequences* (New York, 1881), laid out a wonderfully eclectic set of causes for modern "neurasthenia," including both physical and social conditions, though he did not say exactly why overspecialization should be one of them. He was also quite optimistic about the longer-term effects of prosperity and the "law" of evolution and adaption: see ch. 5. Cf. Daniel T. Rodgers, *The Work Ethic in Industrial America, 1850–1920* (Chicago, 1978), ch. 4 ("Play, Repose and Plenty").

27. Jane Addams's paper was first published as "A New Impulse to an Old Gospel" in *Forum* 14 (November 1892), pp. 345–58. It was reprinted as "The Subjective Necessity for Social Settlements," in Henry C. Adams, ed., *Philosophy and Social Progress* (New York, 1893), and excerpted at length in Addams, *Twenty Years at Hull-House* (New York, 1910), ch. 6. Allen F. Davis, *American Heroine: The Life and Legend of Jane Addams* (New York, 1973), pp. 63–65, traces these ideas to Tolstoy and the English settlement movement, while noting that Addams popularized them and applied them specifically to American college-educated women. For somewhat similar concerns about America's "gilded youth," cf. William James, "The Moral Equivalent of War," in James, *Essays on Faith and Morals,* ed. Ralph Barton Perry (New York, 1943). On other strands of Addams's concern with community versus modern atomism, see her essay on George M. Pullman, "A Modern Lear" (1894), reprinted in Christopher Lasch, ed., *The Social Thought of Jane Addams* (Indianapolis, 1965).

28. Ernest Thompson Seton, *Boy Scouts of America: A Handbook of Woodcraft, Scouting and Lifecraft* (New York, 1910), pp. x, xii, 34–38. Shih (note 9 above), ch. 8, gives useful background on the British-born Seton and on related movements, in Britain as well as America. Allen F. Davis (note 27 above) has observed to me that middle-class fears of urban lower-class juvenile delinquency at the time included a belief that the city was sexually overstimulating.

29. Cf. Theodore Roosevelt, *The Strenuous Life: Essays and Addresses* (New York, 1900); John P. Mallan, "Roosevelt, Brooks Adams, and Lea: The Warrior Critique of Business Civilization," *American Quarterly* 8 (1956), pp. 216–30.

30. Despite the similarities between Nordau and Lasch (p. 98 fn.) Jesse Battan has contrasted late nineteenth-century fear of neurasthenia, attributed to "over-civilization and instinctual renunciation," with late twentieth-century fear of *narcissism,* attributed to "under-civilization and self-indulgence."

Battan, "The 'New Narcissism' in 20th Century America," *Journal of Social History,* 17 (1983), p. 211. On degeneration and the 'woman question,' cf. Charlotte Perkins Gilman, *Women and Economics: The Economic Factor Between Men and Women as a Factor in Social Evolution* (Boston, 1898), esp. pp. 25, 44–46 in the 1966 Harper paperback; Aileen S. Kraditor, *Ideas of the Woman Suffrage Movement, 1880–1920* (New York, 1981), pp. 117–19; Carroll Smith-Rosenberg and Charles Rosenberg, "The Female Animal," *Journal of American History* 60 (1973–74), pp. 332–56; also Justice David J. Brewer's opinion for the Supreme Court majority in *Muller* v. *Oregon* (1908), p. 270 in Hofstadter (note 22 above).

31. A close reading of Frederick Jackson Turner's papers on the frontier reveals some ambivalence toward it and toward the future; he hoped pioneer individualism would "enlarge" into a more public-spirited democracy. See his papers of 1893 and 1903, reprinted in George Rogers Taylor, ed., *The Turner Thesis* (Boston, 1956), chaps. 1, 2, esp. p. 33; also Turner's letter to Carl Becker (January 12, 1945), in Michael G. Kammen, ed., *What Is the Good of History? Selected Letters of Carl L. Becker* (Ithaca, 1973), pp. 333–34. Higham (note 23 above) refers to anxieties among farmers and others about pressure on land supply and opportunity in the late 1880s and early '90s.

32. Cf. Frank Norris, *Moran of the Lady Letty: An Adventure off the California Coast* (New York, 1898); Norris, *McTeague: A Story of San Francisco* (1899); Norris, *Vandover and the Brute* (New York, 1914; probably written before 1897); Jack London, *The Call of the Wild* (New York, 1903); London, *The Sea-Wolf* (New York, 1904). In *Sister Carrie* (New York, 1900), Theodore Dreiser made explicit comparisons between a man's physical and mental growth and decay and the career of economic fortunes: see pp. 338–39 in the 1981 Penguin paperback. Around 1900, the Siegel and Cooper department store declared that "laxity . . . may be your downfall and ruination for life." David J. Rothman and Sheila M. Rothman, eds., *Sources of the American Social Tradition* (New York, 1975), vol. II, p. 16.

33. Oswald Garrison Villard, *Fighting Years: Memoirs of a Liberal Editor* (New York, 1939), p. 324. Valerie Watt, "Our Kind of Self: Autobiography and American Progressives" (Ph.D. diss., American Studies, University of Sussex, Eng., 1987), ch. 6, discusses this statement in relation to other Progressives' fear of European contamination in World War I. John Thompson, "Woodrow Wilson and World War I: A Reappraisal," *Journal of American Studies* 19 (1985), pp. 325–48, explores similar attitudes in Wilson and the press before U.S. entry into the war.

34. See, for example, the poster put out by U.S. Steel in the 1919 strike, reproduced in Henry Pelling, *American Labor* (Chicago, 1960), facing p. 95.

35. Madison Grant, *The Passing of the Great Race, or the Racial Basis of European History* (New York, 1916; rev. ed., 1918), preface by Henry F.

Osborn (a zoology professor); Lothrop Stoddard, *The Rising Tide of Color, Against White-World Supremacy* (New York, 1920), introduction by Madison Grant. Despite their American stress on immigration and ethnicity, these writers also reflected a European interest in the rise and fall of civilizations that was not always racist. Cf. Arthur James Balfour, *Decadence* (Cambridge, Eng., 1908); Oswald Spengler, *The Decline of the West*, 2 vols. (German original, 1918, 1922; English transl., 1926).

36. On Klan organization, see Rothman and Rothman (note 32 above), ch. 17 (Klan documents and reports). It shows among other things the explicit appeals both to military hierarchy/obedience and to egalitarian fellowship. On the Klan's widespread influence and constituencies (middle-class and lower-class, urban as well as rural), see Arnold S. Rice, *The Ku Klux Klan in American Politics* (Washington, D.C., 1962), and Kenneth T. Jackson, *The Ku Klux Klan in the City, 1915–1930* (New York, 1967). Hofstadter (note 3 above), pp. 32–35, argues that Klan ritualism resembled aspects of Catholicism and reflected an old tendency of "paranoid" movements to project "unacceptable traits onto the enemy by parroting their style." On the racist use of romantic medievalism and Gothic primitivism to distance modern Europe, see Wilkinson (note 9 above), pp. 97–98.

37. Quotations are mainly taken from the Klan's Imperial Wizard and Emperor Hiram Wesley Evans, "The Klan's Fight for Americanism," *North American Review* 223 (1926–27), pp. 33–63; but I have also used Paul M. Winter, *What Price Tolerance?* (Hewlett, L.I., 1928), excerpted in Davis (note 3 above), pp. 240–47. Both writers assumed that "old-stock, Nordic Americans" were Protestant, thus ignoring the many Catholic Germans, etc. They also used the term "mongrelized" (versus racial purity), yet denied that the "melting pot" had melted people together.

38. Daniel Horowitz, *The Morality of Spending: Attitudes Toward the Consumer Society in America, 1875–1940* (Baltimore, 1985), chaps. 5–7, explores anxieties about consumption and poverty, 1900s–20s. John S. Whitley, "A Touch of Disaster: Fitzgerald Before Spengler," in A. Robert Lee, ed., *Scott Fitzgerald: The Promise of Life* (London, 1988), notes the influence of Oswald Spengler and nineteenth-century ideas of decline in Fitzgerald's concern with consumption in the twenties, especially drinking and smoking.

39. Roland Marchand, *Advertising the American Dream: Making Way for Modernity, 1920–1940* (Berkeley, 1985), pp. 140–48, 154, 223–28.

40. Cf. Robert S. McElvaine, *The Great Depression: America 1929–1940* (New York, 1984), chaps. 8, 9; Frances Fox Piven and Richard A. Cloward, *Poor People's Movements: Why They Succeed, How They Fail* (New York, 1977), chaps. 2, 3; John Steinbeck, *The Grapes of Wrath* (New York, 1939); Warren French, ed., *Companion to* The Grapes of Wrath (New York, 1963). Steinbeck's great novel has much on the fear of falling apart at the family level

(Ma Joad's drive to hold a dwindling family together) and explicitly discusses the growth of property from initially enhancing a man to owning and diminishing him. See pp. 31–32 in the 1955 Bantam paperback; cf. MacLeish (note 41 below).

41. On Alvin Hansen in relation to Britain's Keynes and America's Turner, see Donald Winch, *Economics and Policy* (London, 1969), pp. 246–49. John Whitley points out to me that fear of entropy (a listless state of unused energy) was a literary theme in the 1930s: see, e.g., Nathanael West, *The Day of the Locust* (New York, 1939). See also Archibald MacLeish's poem of 1937, *The Land of the Free* (New York, 1938), published with collected photographs of the Depression. The poem moves from the loss of old freedoms, which resided in free and fertile land, to questioning the initial value of those freedoms—of any freedoms not based directly on people. The poem thus moves beyond Turner, and beyond the fear of falling away to querying the initial standards.

42. Franklin D. Roosevelt, second inaugural address (January 20, 1937), reprinted in Roosevelt, *Public Papers and Addresses,* ed. Samuel I. Rosenman (New York, 1930), vol. VI, p. 3. My quotation deviates slightly from this text in following the spoken words on tape. The inner quotation, "each age . . .," is from Arthur O'Shaugnessy's "Ode" of 1874: "We are the music makers . . ." Other quotations above are taken from this address, and from Roosevelt's speech accepting renomination for President (June 27, 1936), in Roosevelt, ibid., vol. V, pp. 230–36. Roosevelt's first inaugural (1933) also touched on the fear of falling apart, stressing modern interdependence and the need for a united assault on the country's problems. The reference above to a road ahead recurs in modern presidential campaign speeches and inaugurals, as does the "crossroads of destiny" image. Roosevelt's use of Revolutionary images against corporate monopoly resembles Robert La Follette's rhetoric in his speech accepting the Progressive party nomination in 1924. See Hofstadter (note 22 above), pp. 333–35.

43. On public attitudes to federal spending and New Deal measures, see *The Gallup Poll: Public Opinion 1935–1971* (New York, 1972), vol. I, polls October 20, 1935; January 12, 1936; and several in May 1936. Also *Fortune* polls given by McElvaine (note 40 above), p. 222. Frank Knox is quoted by Arthur M. Schlesinger, Jr., *The Age of Roosevelt,* vol. III, *The Politics of Upheaval* (Boston, 1960), p. 606 in the Sentinel paperback; also p. 529 ("Europeanized Regimentation").

44. Godfrey Hodgson, *In Our Time: America from World War II to Nixon* (New York, 1976), ch. 4 ("The Ideology of the Liberal Consensus"), informatively and brilliantly exaggerates the satisfaction of educated Americans with domestic conditions in this period. He tries too much to fit one "liberalism" over the whole, and he largely overlooks criticisms of culture and

character. Richard H. Pells, *The Liberal Mind in a Conservative Age: American Intellectuals in the 1940s and 1950s* (New York, 1985), chaps. 3, 4, is a corrective. On theories of "class convergence" held at the time, see Paul Blumberg, *Inequality in an Age of Decline* (New York, 1980), pp. 13–18. Donald Meyer, *The Positive Thinkers* (New York, 1965), pp. 171–72, observes that postwar "lamentations [over] loss of spirit" focused on young men entering business, whereas similar fears of decadence in the twenties and thirties concentrated on manual workers, allegedly softened by high wages or relief. Meg Greenfield, "The Great American Morality Play," *Reporter* (June 8, 1961), pp. 13–18, itemizes various scandals, from cheating to kickbacks, and discusses the cycle of lament they triggered among leaders and commentators. James Gilbert explores the period's exaggerated concern about juvenile delinquency in *A Cycle of Outrage: America's Reaction to the Juvenile Delinquent* (New York, 1986). On America's "payola mentality," see John F. Kennedy's 1960 speech (quoted in note 58 below). On "privatism," etc., Philip E. Jacob, *Changing Values in College: An Exploratory Study of the Impact of College Teaching* (New York, 1957); John Kenneth Galbraith, *The Affluent Society* (Boston, 1958), esp. ch. 18; and again, Vance Packard, *The Waste Makers* (New York, 1960), ch. 20.

45. Cold War anxieties showed up in the very titles of magazine articles: see *Reader's Guide to Periodical Literature* under "Morale, National" and "U.S. Moral Conditions." According to a recent survey, Americans think Russians work harder than they, despite the supposed incentive system of capitalism: Adam Clymer, "Polling Americans," *New York Times Magazine* (November 10, 1985), p. 37. Wilkinson (note 9 above), p. 174, n. 83, gives examples of strenuous welcome for the Cold War's challenge. *Goals for Americans,* the report of the U.S. President's Commission on National Goals (Washington, D.C., 1960), joined five reports, 1958–60, by The Rockefeller Brothers Fund, combined into *Prospect for America: The Rockefeller Panel Reports* (New York, 1961): they included institutional policies as well as values. *NSC 68,* the crucial defense policy document of the National Security Council (Washington, D.C., April 14, 1950; mainly written by Paul Nitze), starts with a black-and-white list of Soviet and U.S. goals and values, but later contradicts itself on American cohesion: "dangerous and divisive trends," yet "a unique degree of unity." See Thomas H. Etzold and John Lewis Gaddis, eds., *Containment: Documents on American Policy and Strategy, 1945–1950* (New York, 1978), pp. 389, 402. John Foster Dulles's statements in the late 1940s and early '50s show a growing concern with American betrayal of its religious origins and a consequent loss of dynamism. (I am grateful here to Jerre Bridges, " 'A Righteous and Dynamic Faith': John Foster Dulles and the Early Years of the Cold War," undergraduate paper, American Studies, University of North Carolina, 1987). On fact and opinion in the Korea POW affair, see

H. H. Wubben, "American Prisoners of War in Korea," *American Quarterly* 22 (1970), pp. 3–19. The matter was cited as late as 1960 by Vance Packard in his indictment of American culture and character (note 44 above).

46. The quotation from *NSC 68* is in Etzold and Gaddis (note 45 above), pp. 412–13. Chester Bowles's statement is in his book *Ambassador's Report* (New York, 1954), postscript. See also his view of imperial failures in history, in Bowles, *A View from New Delhi: Selected Speeches and Writings* (New Haven, 1969), pp. 264–65; from a 1965 article. William J. Lederer and Eugene Burdick, *The Ugly American* (New York, 1958), stressed anticommunism more than did Bowles's book of 1954, but they had a similar view of communists in Asia. Christopher Thorne, *American Political Culture and the Asian Frontier* (London, 1988), gives much relevant material, including statements by American officials and others. In Alaska in the late fifties, as at other times, both supporters and opponents of the proposed Arctic wildlife range attached their own concepts of America's "last frontier" to a rhetorical concern with preserving American "vitality." Peter Allan Coates, "The Trans-Alaska Pipeline Controversy in Historical Perspective" (Ph.D. diss., History, Cambridge University, 1988), ch. 3, sec. 3.

47. Although Sinclair Lewis's novels about conformity enjoyed large sales, they were published at a time of big-city experimentalism; their middle America did not seem to be a future. 'Conformity' was more a buzzword in the fifties. Cf. Lewis, *Main Street* (New York, 1919) and *Babbitt* (New York, 1922); also George Jean Nathan and H. L. Mencken, *A Contribution Toward the Interpretation of the American Mind* (New York, 1920).

48. From very different corners in the 1950s, Sloan Wilson's widely read novel, *The Man in the Gray Flannel Suit* (New York, 1955), and Norman Mailer's essay on "The White Negro" (1957), defended personal life and integrity against the psychic demands of corporate America. See Mailer, *Advertisements for Myself* (New York, 1961), pp. 269–90 in the Panther paperback. For left-wing criticisms of social relations in the fifties, see C. Wright Mills, *White Collar* (New York, 1951), and Pells (note 44 above), pp. 198, 428. On Appalachian Volunteers (AVs), see Marie Tyler McGraw, "Staying On: Poverty Warriors in West Virginia," *Journal of American Culture* 8 (1985), pp. 93–103. AVs came from quite a wide range of middle-class family backgrounds, but had often found community in activist movements. For many (not all) of them, nature was an important part of Appalachia's appeal to them; they wanted to live in a pastoral community and find there an "*unconditional* love" (cf. Margaret Mead). In a lecture at Sussex University, England (June 6, 1985), McGraw went on to say that many AVs had taken social science courses at college. There they were influenced by notions of 'alienation' in modern mass society (not just America), which had become an academic concern in the fifties and early

sixties. Cf. Harry McPherson, *A Political Education* (Boston, 1972), pp. 301–2; also Erich Fromm's seminal book, *Escape from Freedom* (New York, 1941), esp. ch. 5, sec. 3. Whereas Mills and others suggested that commercially driven conforming isolated people psychologically, Fromm put it the other way about: people conformed compulsively because they felt alone and powerless. Both, of course, could be true: a vicious circle. Writing subsequently about William Whyte's Park Forest suburb, Erich Fromm argued more that its conformism "alienated" people from *themselves,* from their deepest and most individual feelings, than that it was not a real community. His solutions to man's "alienation" by capitalism and modern organization did, however, include "communitarian socialism." In reply, Whyte denied that one could have intensive community without conformity. See Whyte, "The Transients," *Fortune* (series, May, June, July, August 1953); Fromm, *The Sane Society* (New York, 1955), pp. 110–21, 154–63, 283ff., 306ff. in the Routledge paperback; Whyte, *The Organization Man* (New York, 1956), pp. 361–62 in the Simon and Schuster paperback.

49. Students for a Democratic Society, "Port Huron Statement" (1962), was mainly written by Tom Hayden and is reprinted in Judith Clavier Albert and Stewart Edward Albert, eds., *The Sixties Papers: Documents of a Rebellious Decade* (New York, 1984), pp. 176–96. Its beautifully balanced prose is curiously similar to that of George Kennan, who criticized the new left in Kennan et al., *Democracy and the Student Left* (Boston, 1968). James Miller, *"Democracy Is in the Streets": From Port Huron to the Siege of Chicago* (New York, 1987), tells about the Statement's writing and background. The Statement said little about what caused or who controlled the power system it attacked, beyond very cursory references to "business elites" and "corporations" and rather more on southern bigots. Nixon's acceptance speech at the Republican National Convention (August 8, 1968) is reprinted in Arthur M. Schlesinger, Jr., and Fred Israel, eds., *History of American Presidential Elections* (New York, 1985), vol. IX, pp. 3832–40. The image of returning home from the wrong road was repeated in "Bring Our Country Back," Nixon's 'country and western' campaign song; and again, ironically, in George McGovern's speech accepting the Democratic nomination for President in 1972: "come home, America," from Indo-China, racism, exploitation, and waste. See Joe McGinniss, *The Selling of the President 1968* (New York, 1969), pp. 122–24; *New York Times* (July 14, 1972), p. 11.

50. The first annual U.S. trade deficit since 1893 occurred in 1971. A growth in 'two-breadwinner' families and in moonlighting during the 1970s partially offset the drop in real earnings per hour. On trends in incomes and benefits, see Samuel Bowles et al., *Beyond the Waste Land: A Democratic Alternative to Economic Decline* (New York, 1983), ch. 2; Oxford Analytica, *America in Perspective: Major Trends in the United States Through the 1980s*

(New York, 1982, 1986); Steven Greenhouse, on declining incomes, *New York Times* (July 19, 1986); Betsy Morris, "Strapped Yuppies," *Wall Street Journal* (December 17, 1985); Jane Seaberry, on divergent trends, *Washington Post* (January 6, 1987).

51. In the 1970s, surveys generally showed more pessimism about the nation's future than the future of oneself and one's family. In 1978 and '79, a majority thought the national situation (vaguely defined) would be worse in five years time. Surveys from 1979 to 1983, however, found increasing *economic* pessimism about the prospects for one's children, even after the early 1980s recession ended. Yet a survey found in 1982 that Americans claimed to be prouder of their country than did West Europeans and Japanese: Marjorie Hyer, "Poll Finds Americans Most Proud," *International Herald Tribune* (May 20, 1982). On the other findings, see Seymour Martin Lipset, *The First New Nation* (New York, 1963, 1979), pp. v–xiii in the 1979 Norton edition; Blumberg (note 44 above), pp. 253–56; survey in *Psychology Today* (September 1981), pp. 37–38; Everett Carll Ladd, "How Americans See Themselves," *Dialogue* 55 (1982), pp. 6–8; Barry Sussman, on *Washington Post*–ABC News Polls, *Washington Post* (February 21, 1983); David S. Broder et al., interviews and surveys, *Washington Post* (April 23, 1987).

52. Studs Terkel, *American Dreams: Lost and Found* (New York, 1980), pp. 46–50: interview with Gaylord Freeman, retiring chairman of First National Bank of Chicago. Cf. Christopher Lasch, *The Culture of Narcissism* (New York, 1979); Daniel Bell, *The Cultural Contradictions of Capitalism* (New York, 1976; summarized in foreword to 1979 edition).

53. OPEC (Organization of Petroleum Producing Exporting Countries) hiked oil prices by several hundred percent between January 1973 and January 1974.

54. See Dee Brown, *Bury My Heart at Wounded Knee: An Indian History of the American West* (New York, 1971), and various other books in the seventies on frontier violence and racism. Cf. Hodgson (note 44 above), p. 471. The ground was prepared for these by the assassinations and riots of the sixties, which had prompted studies of violence in American history. On mass, popular levels, however, criticisms of U.S. policy in Vietnam seldom took a moral line. This point is well documented by Jane Streeter, "The Meaning of Class in the Analysis of Opposition to the Vietnam War," undergraduate paper (Government Department, Smith College, December 1985). By 1971, too, the reduction of U.S. troops there in return for stepped-up bombing had reduced general protest against the war.

55. Edmund Morgan, "Slavery and Freedom: The American Paradox," *Journal of American History* 59 (1972), pp. 5–29; originally given as a presidential address to the Organization of American Historians (1972). Of course Charles A. Beard, *An Economic Interpretation of the Constitution of the United*

States (New York, 1913), had long before questioned the disinterested majesty of the Founders.

56. For a range of positions, see Arnold A. Rogow, *The Dying Light: A Searching Look at America Today* (New York, 1975); Blumberg (note 44 above), pp. 231–53; Joseph Epstein, *Ambition: The Secret Passion* (New York, 1980); and the authors reviewed on pp. 27–38. On attitudes to the environment, see Shih (note 9 above), ch. 10.

57. Quoted by Fred Barbach and Barry Sussman, *Washington Post* (July 15, 1979).

58. Carter's television speech was printed in the *Washington Post* (July 16, 1979), p. A14. In my study of party convention acceptance speeches, 1948–80, I found they nearly always praised the electorate. In 1960, however, John F. Kennedy declared that a moral "dry rot" (albeit "beginning in Washington") had affected "every corner of America—in the payola mentality, the expense account way of life, the confusion between what is legal and what is right. Too many Americans have lost their way, their will, and their sense of historic purpose." In 1964, the Republicans' Barry Goldwater said, "Our people have followed false prophets." See Schlesinger and Israel (note 49 above), vol. IX, pp. 3543, 3664. Carter's speech, however, made the moral and psychological condition of the people a more dominant theme. For my study of acceptance speeches, see Wilkinson, "Saying Yes," *London Review of Books* 6 (July 19–August 1, 1984), pp. 18–19.

59. *Time,* September 24, 1984; May 23, 1987. Cf. Broder et al. (note 51 above); Stewart Fleming, "A Bear Market in American Dreams," *Financial Times* (London, May 23, 1987). Note also the fear of decline and falling apart in Allan Bloom's *The Closing of the American Mind: How Higher Education Has Failed Democracy and Impoverished the Souls of Today's Students* (New York, 1987): the book reached top place for nonfiction in the *New York Times* weekly survey of bookstores.

Epilogue

1. An exception to the tendency to focus studies of psychic costs on the middle class is Richard Sennett and Jonathan Cobb, *The Hidden Injuries of Class* (New York, 1972), a study of working-class lives and feelings. See also some of the studies by Robert Coles; but the main exception is the literature on black Americans.

2. Cf. David Halle, *America's Working Man: Work, Home, and Politics Among Blue-Collar Property Owners* (Chicago, 1984), chaps. 9, 12; Thomas Ferguson and Joel Rogers, "The Myth of America's Turn to the Right," *Atlantic Monthly* 257 (May 1986), pp. 43–53. On the nature of U.S. covert operations abroad, see Gregory F. Treverton, *Covert Action: The Limits of Intervention in the Postwar World* (New York, 1987).

3. On the failure and terrible human costs of this policy, see William Shawcross, *Kissinger, Nixon and the Destruction of Cambodia* (London, 1979; rev. ed., 1986). An appendix contains rebuttals and counterrebuttals by Peter Rodman for Kissinger and by Shawcross.

4. Reagan's statement is quoted from his State of the Union Address (January 27, 1987).

5. Cf. Ella Leffland, *Rumors of Peace* (New York, 1979). On isolationism and lack of education, surveys have shown that until well into the Vietnam War (late 1968 or '69), less-educated people were more apt to agree that "U.S. involvement in Vietnam was a mistake." *Gallup Opinion Weekly* (October 1969), p. 15.

6. George Washington, Farewell Address (1796), in Daniel Boorstin, ed., *The American Primer* (Chicago, 1966), vol. I, p. 204.

Index

Education, 10, 18, 24, 33, 39, 43–44, 46, 53, 154. *See also* Colleges

Egalitarianism, equality, inequality, 15–16, 21, 22, 25, 34, 47, 114; and college faculty, 67; in nineteenth century, 91, 93–94, 95–96, 97; in 'new left' ideas, 107; and Edmund Morgan on slavery, 109

Egocentrism, egoism, 1, 13, 31, 41, 42–45, 48, 49; and Christopher Lasch, 31–33, David Riesman, 19, 33–35; Daniel Yankelovich, 35–36; at turn of century, 98–99

Eisenhower, Dwight, Commission on National Goals, 105; Council on Physical Fitness, 79

Elections, U.S. presidential, 10, 47; in 1936, 82, 103–4; in 1960, 80–81, 104; in 1968, 82, 85, 108; in 1976, 84; in 1980, 36

Election sermons, 89

'Energy crisis,' 18, 109, 110–11

Enlightenment, 59

Environment. *See* Ecological concerns

Erikson, Erik, 9, 120–21

Ethnicity, 7, 11, 13, 34–35; and four fears, 95, 100–101

Europe, attitudes toward, 14, 47, 69, 73, 77; and nature, 83; and early Puritans, 81; and Revolution, 89; in early Republic, 90–91; and Civil War, 93; and nineteenth-century industrialism, 96; in early twentieth century, 98, 99–101

Evangelism. *See* Puritanism; Revivalism

'Exceptionalism,' American, 11, 18, 45

Expansiveness, 15, 46. *See also* Dynamism; Fear of winding down

"Expressive individualism" (Bellah), 37, 68

"False consciousness" (Reich), 28, 49. *See also* Authenticity

Falwell, Jerry, 79

Family, 13, 14, 35, 44–45; achievement pressures in, 14, 15, 30, 31, 42; and generations, 64–65, 70, 76–77; isolation of, 29, 30; structures and styles of, 17, 18, 27, 30, 32, 33, 39, 51–52, 107; threats to, 31, 32–33, 39, 49, 51–52; in 1830s revivalism, 61–62;

Family (*cont.*)
on overland trails, 63; and 'Okies,' 102

Fashion, 17, 39, 42

Fear of being owned, 2, 4, 12, 71–75, 118; in American-character studies, 48–49, 51–53; history of, 87–112; in foreign policy; 117; in social policy, 114

Fear of falling apart, 2, 4, 12, 71–72, 75–77, 117; in American-character studies, 48, 49–50, 51–53; history of, 87–112; in foreign policy, 105–6, 117; in social policy, 114

Fear of falling away, 2, 4, 12, 71–72, 79–82, 83–86 pass., 117; in American-character studies, 48, 50–53; history of, 87–112; in foreign policy, 105–6, 114–17 pass.; in social policy, 114

Fear of winding down, 2, 4, 12, 71–72, 77–79, 80–81, 117; in American-character studies, 48, 50–53; history of, 87–88, 90–112, 134; in foreign policy, 105–6, 114–17 pass.; in social policy, 114

Feminism, 34, 55, 65, 66; and fear of being owned, 74–75; and fear of winding down, 98–99

Fender, Stephen, 73, 89–90

Ferguson, Kathy E., 55

Feudalism, 15, 18, 24

Finney, Charles, 60–61

Florida, 47–48

Fonda, Jane, 79

Foreign observers of America, 5, 8, 45, 46, 47. *See also under specific names*

Foreign relations, U.S., 8, 13, 81; and four fears, reviewed, 114–17; 'realpolitik' and 'universalist,' 115; in early twentieth century, 99–100; in Cold War views, 105–6, 113–17; and 'Irangate,' 85, 112n

Fortune magazine, 19

Founding Fathers, 81, 90, 91, 94, 105, 109

480, The (Burdick), 10

Four fears. *See* Fear of being owned; Fear of falling apart; Fear of falling away; Fear of winding down

Stetson College Library